gratuitous annotation ou ?

D1736459

Tales of
Sonoma County
REFLECTIONS ON A GOLDEN AGE

A day at the ranch with Dr. Shipley's son Billy (left), another young man (most likely Albert Larsen), and Dr. Shipley himself (right).

On the Cover: Dr. Shipley's son Billy and nephew Albert Larsen enjoy play time in Cloverdale.

Tales of
Sonoma County
REFLECTIONS ON A GOLDEN AGE

Dr. William C. Shipley

Compiled by The Sonoma County Historical Society

TEMPUS

Published by Arcadia Publishing,
an imprint of Tempus Publishing, Inc.
2 Cumberland Street
Charleston, SC 29401

Printed in Great Britain.

Library of Congress Catalog Card Number: 00-111910

For all general information contact Arcadia Publishing at:
Telephone 843-853-2070
Fax 843-853-0044
E-Mail sales@arcadiapublishing.com

For customer service and orders:
Toll-Free 1-888-313-2665

Visit us on the internet at http://www.arcadiaimages.com

Around 1910, the Sotoyome Band included, from left to right, Ed Fenno, Professor A.C. "Pop" Smith, John Fay, an unidentified individual, Louis B. Proomis, another unidentified individual, Charles Butler, and Ben Ware. (Courtesy Vivian Hall, Healdsburg Museum collection.)

CONTENTS

The stage at Skaggs Springs. (Courtesy Healdsburg Museum collection.)

Tales of Sonoma County *was first printed in 1965*
by The Sonoma County Historical Society,
by permission of Mrs. William Shipley and the Healdsburg Tribune,
where the articles originally appeared in 1938.

The photographs contained herein
appear courtesy of the Shipley family and the Healdsburg Museum.

The Sonoma County Historical Society gratefully acknowledges
the assistance of the Healdsburg Museum,
especially Director Marie Djordjevich and Curator Holly Hoods.

INTRODUCTION

Dr. Shipley was born in Healdsburg, California, on June 2, 1872, the son of John C. and Josephine Schermerhorn Shipley. His grandfather, R.J. Shipley, searched for gold in the Sierra Nevada in 1849 before settling down as a rancher in Sonoma County. John Shipley joined his father at age nine and taught for more than forty years in the Redwood Empire. He died in 1906.

Dr. Shipley attended schools in Healdsburg and later graduated from the California Medical College in San Francisco in 1900. The school was destroyed in the earthquake and fire in 1906. The young doctor married Anna Hildebrandt, the daughter of San Francisco pioneers Mr. and Mrs. Henry Hildebrandt, in 1902 in Alameda. On September 25, 1903, they had a son, William Henry Shipley. He spent the first seven years of his medical practice as a surgeon working for mining companies in Calaveras County. In 1907 he moved to Cloverdale, where he practiced for twenty years. He established Cloverdale General Hospital in 1920. In 1927, the Shipley family moved to a home on Third Street in Santa Rosa. Dr. Shipley had offices in the Rosenberg Building and on Mendocino Avenue for many years. His membership in the Sonoma County Medical Society dated from April 9, 1908.

Throughout his life he contributed articles on California history to Bay Area and Redwood Empire newspapers and journals. He was the founding president of the Sonoma County Historical and Museum Society and led a campaign to establish a Sonoma County Museum to preserve records and relics. He was a member of the Sons of the American Revolution and the Native Sons of the Golden West. The doctor was active on the home front during World War II and later was one of the founders of the Sonoma County Blood Bank (SCBB). He retired in 1950 and became director of the SCBB. Dr. Shipley, eighty-eight, died at his home at 700 Third Street on August 12, 1960. His wife died in Lafayette at the age of ninety on October 2, 1967.

The articles in this book, mostly looking back at the early days of Healdsburg history, appeared in the *Healdsburg Tribune* in 1938. The first edition was published in 1965. In her preface to that edition, Fidelia Furber Harlow, an artist and friend, said the following of Dr. Shipley: "He kept abreast of the times and conditions in every sense of the word, as a true American, ever mindful of his country, friends and family . . . In line of professional duties, it is inconceivable to my imagination that a thought of neglect ever entered his mind, regardless of his own personal weariness. In the old horse and buggy days he would travel all night, regardless of climactic conditions, over mountains and streams, when called upon by anyone needing his services. One never felt reluctant to ask his advice, and he was always ready to help in any way he could, always by a smile and cheery word. In his later years, he had many hobbies to occupy his spare time, one of which—he loved to write of incidents of people and places, memories of the past all most interesting and many historic—will stand as a monument of this generation to those who will follow. To my knowledge he was the first one to call a meeting (in 1948) to form a historical society such as this, to create interest and to form a museum for Sonoma County . . . May history not forget our own Dr. Shipley."

It should be remembered that Dr. Shipley wrote about incidents and events that occurred over fifty to one hundred years ago. He was a product of his era and sometimes reflected feelings common then but out of date or even discredited today. Regarding spelling, sentence structure, and word use, an effort was made to retain Dr. Shipley's original writing both in style and in substance unless a failure to update it would result in a lack of clarity for the reader.

—Harry Lapham and Lee Torliatt

RAMBLINGS

As I travel the pathway of life down the western slope toward the setting sun, with hope for the future whatever it may be, it sometimes pays to look back through the vista of years, now over threescore and ten, to those events that have made life a glorious experience.

All of us have our joys and sorrows, our ups and downs, but the pleasures and prosperities of life so far outweigh the evils that they may be forgotten. To us comes thoughts of family and friends, those we have known, loved, and lived with.

As a small boy, to me, my home and parents were the best in all the world and I still think so even in this modern age; not that other parents and other homes were not as good, but to me mine was best, for comfort, security, peace, plenty and love abode therein and were my constant companions. True, on some occasions there were clouds, but they were soon dispelled by the sunshine of understanding and co-operation.

My parents, my grandparents, and two of my great-grandparents were known to me and they all contributed their part in shaping my life for all time. I reverence their memory for they were all true-blue Americans of the old school from both sides of the Mason-Dixon line.

To my descendants and to my sister Nell's son I have tried to impart those sterling virtues handed to me by my ancestors, some of whom helped in the founding of the American colonies and the establishment of these United States.

Without being bigoted or egotistical I believe my family, both past and present and to come, is the best in the whole world, my wife the finest woman and mother now living, my home the best and happiest in the land, my town in which I live the best in the county, my county the best in the state, my state the best in the nation, and my country, the good old U.S.A., the best of this mundane sphere, even though it could be improved a bit to the betterment of mankind.

Since the year 1900 I have had the pleasure of an extensive and active medical practice which to me has been an experience that cannot be measured in dollars and cents; I have made contacts with others of the human family regardless of race or creed that have been illuminating, among the rich and poor, the sick and the well, and while I might not want to live it all over again, nothing else could replace this grand, intimate association with other humans, for I have found the vast majority to possess true and honest hearts and to be appreciative of friendship and good will.

We all get out of life what we put in and are able to give, whether it is something very great or just a little bit. While I have only been able to contribute in a small way I have received from life many blessings, a great deal of satisfaction and I wish to thank my family and friends for what I have received. It is not so much the intrinsic value of a gift as it is the spirit in which it is given that counts.

I am thankful to my Creator for a strong, sturdy body and good health which have served me well in all work which I love to do.

William Shipley as a young M.D.

One: The Way It Was

Roads and Transportation. In the early days the roads in Sonoma County and the streets of our growing communities were dirt and gravel—mostly dirt—which in summer were very dusty and during the rainy season were from a few inches to a foot deep in mud of many consistencies.

In summertime most travelers wore cotton and linen dusters to protect their clothing from the dust and in the winter waterproof slickers or oil skins and they applied plenty of oil or mutton tallow to their shoes or boots to keep water out and the feet dry.

Many travelled by horseback, some few used ox carts, modified covered wagons for hauling freight, lumber wagons, farm wagons of many kinds, buckboards, Petaluma carts, carriages, surreys, with and without the fringe around the top, and many Concord stagecoaches.

There were many types of one-, two-, three-, and four-horse vehicles in use and on rare occasions, pack trains. A spiked team consisted of three animals, two hitched to the wagon as wheelers with one in front hitched by a singletree to the tip of the wagon pole. Such a team required four reins to drive them, the same as a four-horse team. In some cases teams of six to twelve or more animals were in use. When the teams were composed of more than eight animals, a jerk line was used which was fastened to the bridle of the nigh lead horse or mule. A jockey stick connected this animal to its mate on the off side so they could act as a unit and respond to commands of the driver, who was mounted on the nigh wheeler.

In the '70s, when I was a small boy living with my folks on a ranch at the head of Oat Valley just three miles north of Cloverdale on Boonville Road, which in those days went straight up the bed of the canyon and in places was so steep it was difficult for some teams to pull the heavy loads of freight up the grade to the Mendocino County line, W.D. Sink, a young man whose parents lived in the valley, did a good business helping such teams up the steep grade with a team of four big draft horses. He would hitch his booster team to the end of the chain with a clevis, mount his nigh rear horse, and up the grade they would go, for a reasonable financial consideration. When the crest of the grade was reached, he would detach his team and come back down the hill to the foot of the grade near Alder Glen Springs to wait for another customer.

C.E. Proctor's team in front of the Russian River Flag office on Center Street, 1872.

Speaking of Alder Glen Springs, my grandfather, R.J. Shipley, discovered them in the early '70s and my mother named them. For many years they were known as Shipley's Springs.

As a boy, I saw teams of from six to eight big bulls on Boonville Road and in the '80s, when living in Healdsburg, on rare occasions a bull team from the Joy Mill on Mill Creek would be anchored to the hitching chain about the plaza. For logging in the redwoods many bull teams were used up to the advent of power-driven tractors and cats.

CROPS. From the earliest days, cattle, horses, mules, hogs, sheep, and a few goats were the principal animal products, with wheat, corn, oats, barley, stock beets, and pumpkins for stock feed and domestic use, along with fruit and garden vegetables. Grapes and the production of good dry wines was another early industry, with hops making up a secondary crop.

As the climate in summer was warmer in those days, corn grew tall, and watermelons, pumpkins, and squashes grew gigantic—some so large it took two men to load them into a farm wagon. Hundreds of acres of tall field corn grew in many parts of the county. Many farmers would plant every fifth row in their corn to cow pumpkins, while others planted whole fields to pumpkins and squashes to be stored for the winter stock feed for cattle and hogs.

In the dry, hot days of fall, after the crops had been harvested, small whirlwinds would frequently be seen crossing a field or coming down the dusty roads; when they crossed a corn field they would lift dust, dried corn leaves, and other detritus in a spinning mass high in the air. They were spectacular, but did no harm for they were only miniature cyclones. The faster they would spin, the higher into the sky they mounted.

In those days nearly every farmer raised a few hogs, had a smokehouse, and cured their own hams and bacon. Some would jerk and dry beef, and make corned beef and pork for the winter's use. Corn cobs were used as fuel to make the necessary smoke. Corn was shelled by hand or by horse-power shellers and in cases where the crop was small, by hand, rubbing two ears together, or with a corn cob or by placing a spade or shovel upside down over the edge of a tub or half barrel, the operator sitting stride of the handle to hold it in place. The corn was shelled by drawing the ear across the edge of the spade from heel to tip, which caused the kernels to come off and fall into the receptacle. This process was repeated until all the corn was removed from the cob. Bushels and bushels of corn would be shelled in this manner.

Many farmers killed and dressed their own beef and mutton, sharing with the neighbors their excess; their neighbors would do so in turn. In this way a supply of fresh meat was maintained as there was no means of refrigeration outside the old-fashioned underground cellars. To keep milk and butter in good condition, many housewives would put them in a bucket and lower them down into an open well.

HAY. Most farmers stowed their hay loose in big barns. The hay was sprinkled with stock salt as it was placed in the hay mow to keep it from molding and make it more edible by the stock. This also prevented spontaneous combustion. Some would, after filling their barn, make great stacks on high ground and let the stock feed at will. A few farmers baled their hay with the old fashioned horse-powered hay press, tying the bale with bale rope. These bales were not compact and solid as is the hay baled by modern high-powered lightning car presses, but they served the purpose and made good sweet hay.

THE THRASHING CREWS. As there were thousands of acres of wheat, oats, and barley to be thrashed every year before the rains set in, there were between eight and ten thrashing crews and outfits in Sonoma County, scattered from Cloverdale in the north, to Petaluma in the south, and to Sonoma in the east. Shelford Bros. in the Cloverdale area and Toombs Bros. in the Healdsburg section are well remembered.

The thrashing outfit consisted of a straw burning engine, horse drawn, with a single large tube through the center of the boiler in which to burn the straw to generate steam when operating. A thrasher that thrashed and separated the grain from the straw, fanned and cleaned the grain from the chaff, pouring the cleaned grain out of a chute at one side into sacks and the straw out another chute at the far end of the thrasher to be used as fuel for the engine. One man would be kept busy replacing empty sacks for the full ones and sewing the full ones when the machine was operating. Another man would be occupied stoking straw into the fire box to keep up steam.

There was a cook wagon in which to prepare hearty meals and feed the crew; two or more header wagons that had large beds with one side high and the other low in which to haul the sheaves of grain from the field to thrasher; a buckboard or cart to go for supplies and trail the water cart, which was a large barrel or tank on two wheels in which to transport water for the cook, the crew, and for the steam engine. All vehicles were animal drawn, usually by horses or mules.

The crew was composed of eight to ten men and they carried their bed rolls with them, sleeping on piles of straw under the stars. When moving from ranch to ranch, this outfit made quite a cavalcade of six to eight vehicles, ten to twelve animals, and eight to ten men. It was a great life, full of hard work and some fun.

This was all before the days of the combined harvester, for wheat, oats, and barley ceased to be commercial crops just before the invention of combines and the old-time thrashing outfits went out of business and became ancient history.

Other farm machinery at that time included single and gang plows, clod mashers, harrows, cultivators, hand- and horse-drawn planters and seeders, hay rakes, buck rakes, McCormick reapers, reapers and binders, sickles, scythes, cradles, and on small ranches, a few old-fashioned flails.

THE BLACKSMITH SHOPS. Before the motorization of wheeled vehicles and farm machinery, there were literally thousands of horses and mules and a few oxen used as draft animals in Sonoma County, which necessitated many blacksmith shops or smithies where these animals could be shod, tires shrunk, wheeled vehicles and farm machinery made or repaired, plow points sharpened, etc.

Ox shoes came in pairs for the right and left sides of their cloven hoofs. Mule shoes differed in shape from horse shoes and all came in a variety of weights, light, medium, and heavy, and about seven sizes from small ones for small horses to the great big heavy ones for Clydesdale and other large horses.

In the very early days, many blacksmiths made their shoes by hand from bar iron or steel and, in some cases, made their horse shoe nails from Norway iron. A horse shoe nail had to have a point beveled to one side or it could not be driven into the hoof and come out at the right level to be clinched. The shoeing of animals was an art in which many blacksmiths of that day excelled.

The features of a smithy consisted of a forge and bellows, a big anvil, slack tub, a whole flock of hammers, including a special farriers hammer to drive and clinch the horse shoe nails, flatters, hollows and rounds, cold and hot chisels, tongs with which to handle the hot iron and shoes, punches, rasps, files, paring knives to shape the hoofs, horse shoe nails of several sizes, a tire upsetter to shrink tires, a blacksmith's vise, and a leather apron or two.

From left to right, Mr. and Mrs. Charles York, an unidentified man, Mrs. Frank Cummings, two unidentified men, Elizabeth Cummings (later Mrs. George Waterman), and Luelle Cummings (later Mrs. L.S. Smith). The York blacksmith shop was operated by brothers Gus and Charles York at the corner of West and Piper Streets between 1885 and 1890.

The glowing coals, the flying sparks in the forge, the ringing anvil when struck by the heavy hammer—all this was an inspiring sight and music to one's ears, bringing to mind the poem *The Village Blacksmith*.

Many of the large farms had their own smithy for emergency work and some farmers were quite skilled in the art of blacksmithing. Every town in the county had one or more blacksmith and carriage shops, and smithies were even located at some of the crossroads.

THE LIVERY STABLES. From the earliest days and up to the invention of motor transportation, every community had one or more livery stables where most any kind of one-, two-, or four-horse rigs could be hired by the day or week as necessity demanded.

Some stables had twenty to sixty or more horses, depending on the size of the town and the demand. These institutions prided themselves on their snappy turnouts. Their rigs were kept in perfect condition, their horses were clipped and polished or, rather, groomed to perfection; the harness ornamented to please the eye and the whole outfit, when it went prancing out on display, made a gorgeous show.

Many gay young blades of that day would take their lady friends out for a drive on Sunday afternoon in all this grandeur. The demand for rigs was so heavy that many swains had a standing order, or had to engage rigs several days in advance of the anticipated date with the girl of their choice. It was all very flashy, great sport and, for the liveryman, a profitable business. The liverymen, like the blacksmiths, were prosperous pillars of the community in which they lived and operated.

Horsemen gather in front of the Sotoyome Stables after a Fourth of July parade.

THE GRISTMILLS. The old-fashioned water-powered gristmills were an early day necessity in Sonoma County and on up into the '70s and mid-'80s. They were located on some living stream not far from a good road accessible to the public, and served the community by grinding wheat into flour, corn into meal and cracked corn, and crushing oats and barley for stock feed.

East of Cloverdale on Sulphur Creek was one with a gigantic shot wheel driven by water flumed down the canyon from a dam about two miles up that stream. The mill and flume have been demolished years ago, but part of the dam still remains. Out on Mill Creek west of Healdsburg a grand old mill stood that served the public for many years; it, too, has disappeared. Another old gristmill operated for many years on Sausal Creek out in Alexander Valley, but like all the rest of those historic monuments to early industry, it has crumbled into dust and is but a faded memory of a glorious past.

Many of the pioneer day sawmills were powered by falling water running over a great wheel twenty to forty feet in diameter. For pay, the miller took a percentage of the grist for his services, the amount depending upon the amount of grain to be ground and the locality. The flour and meal of those days was not highly refined as is our modern product, but it made good wholesome food and gave a flavor to bread not to be found in food today, for it contained all the life-giving elements and vitamins of good whole grain.

THE STAGE LINES. From the 1850s to the 1880s, and as late as 1920, horse-drawn stagecoaches of from six to sixteen passenger capacity were in use as common carriers in Sonoma County. They transported passengers, and many carried mail and express which, in the early days of occasional road agents, necessitated mounting a Wells-Fargo Shot Gun Messenger atop the stage. He was not only armed with a double barreled, sawed off shotgun loaded with buck shot, but also carried a side arm, a good old Colt 45 six gun in his belt.

The Concord coach, with its very comfortable body suspended on the running gear with heavy sole leather straps built up of layers to two to three inches in thickness and about four inches in width instead of springs, gave the coach when loaded and in motion, a fore and aft and side to side rocking motion that was delightful. The hubs and axles were so constructed with a bit of play so as to give a clucking sound when traveling, which was almost musical.

Before the Donahue Railroad started north from Tiburon, all travelers into this territory, unless they had their own transportation, had to come by steamer from San Francisco to Petaluma. From there many stage lines branched out to different sections of the county and on into Lake and Mendocino Counties.

In 1872 the railroad reached Cloverdale, which was the end of rail until about the mid-'80s, when it moved on north to Ukiah. During this period, six stages left Cloverdale daily for the Geysers, Lakeport, Ukiah, the West Coast, and all points north. Where traffic was heavy they used six-horse stock and, on the long runs, change stations were located every twelve to fifteen miles, where a fresh team could be acquired and on they would go, for they were supposed to make an average of ten miles per hour.

A stage line from Skaggs Springs to Geyserville made two round trips daily during summer season and one trip in the off season. It was driven for many years by Bob Mason and, in addition to passengers, carried mail, express, and supplies for the hotel at the springs.

The Ledford brothers operated the last horse-drawn stage in Sonoma County out of Cloverdale via Boonville and way stations to Greenwood on the coast. This line was motorized about 1920, but went out of business a few years later.

The old stagecoaches were works of the carriage-makers' art, brilliantly painted, red, green, or yellow, with striping of spokes and bodies; and a canvas covered trunk and baggage rack behind the driver's seat high above the boot in which the mail and express was stowed under the driver's seat. It would be hitched to four or six fine matched stage horses with the harness mounting of silver or brass fixtures, many white or red rings, and a brilliantly colored tassel hanging from the cheek piece of the bridle. The expert driver would be mounted on the box, dressed appropriately and wearing a ten-gallon, pearl-gray John B. Stetson hat, full gauntlet gloves with long braided lash whip in his right hand, mounting a series of silver ferrules on its pliable hickory stock, made a spectacle to cheer the heart and delight the eye.

Such sights are but fond memories of a glorious past and a day that has gone forever.

Most of these events I have had the pleasure of witnessing and my father, who came to Sonoma County as a boy in 1852, told me much about early-day history.

TWO: MEMORIES OF THE CLASSROOM

MY FIRST SCHOOL TEACHER. In the spring of 1880 it was my good fortune at the age of eight to be enrolled in the primary class (eighth grade in those days) of the Healdsburg Public School. I had been taught my ABCs and to count at home. Up to that time my parents lived on a ranch three miles north of Cloverdale. My father taught school and ranched as a side issue, for the pay of teachers was not very great, and many men teachers supplemented their income by preaching, bookkeeping, ranching, or even farm labor. I was so frightened that first morning, and rendered dumb, that Mrs. Allen, the dear old teacher, put me in the chart class until she found that I could read and write and cypher a bit.

Mrs. Allen was quite elderly, and a veteran in the school department. She supported an invalid (?) husband, wore a shaker bonnet, a dark apron with two big pockets, brought her lunch to school in a queer little basket, and among other things always ate two cold soft boiled eggs out of the shells with a spoon, and usually smeared some of the very yellow yolk in the wrinkles at the corners of her mouth, there to dry and remain as a shining light the rest of the afternoon.

There were between seventy and eighty youngsters, ranging from six to sixteen years of age in the two classes of the primary grade, and as there was not desk room for all, unpainted redwood benches having box-like compartments for slates, books, and a seating capacity of six made up the rest of the school furniture.

There was a wire stretched from wall to wall in front of the teacher's desk, on which many spools had been strung. Every fifth spool was black, and with a long pointer, Mrs. Allen would teach the aspirant for knowledge to count by moving the spools from one side to the other, by single spools, by 2s, 3s, 4s, 5s, and 10s.

The chart class was lined up in front of her desk, and with the pointer she would point to the words on the large chart on the wall behind her desk, and the kids would sing the words in unison, C-A-T, cat, D-O-G, dog, R-A-T, rat, and so on until the lesson was completed. A picture of the thing or animal accompanying each word helped make a definite impression on the developing mind. The whole class would sing the multiplication table up to five times twelve was sixty.

After roll call each morning, school was started by reciting the Lord's Prayer, followed by a few school songs such as "The Farmer Boy," "The Rainy Day," or the "Geography Song," which was a great favorite for after enumerating the continents, mountain chains, lakes, rivers, etc., and the fact that the earth was round and like a ball, the chorus ended with "Oceans, gulfs, bays and seas, latitude lines, longitude too, cold polar circles, and all these go through the thousands of green little islands."

For writing material each hopeful had a slate. Some used a damp cloth or sponge to cleanse the same, while many others, especially the boys, just spat on them and rubbed them dry with a rag, their bare hands, or their shirt or coat sleeve, and no one seemed to suffer from microbic infection.

Each morning and noon the water monitors would fill a large bucket with water from the well, and with a tin dipper this was placed on a box in one corner of the room where thirsty students could drink their fill, all from the same dipper, again no casualties.

To be a monitor was a mark of distinction for meritorious conduct, or perfect lessons. We had line monitors, hat monitors, water monitors, etc., so as to have plenty of honorary jobs as a stimulant to scholarship and deportment. Infractions of school regulations were punished by wearing a dunce cap, or whipping with a leather strap, which was freely, and frequently, applied much to the improvement of the rising generation. Punishment was administered for the culprit's own good, and caused the teacher many a heartache.

If a boy or girl had to leave the room, he or she would hold up a hand with two fingers extended and after a nod from the teacher, was permitted to leave the room without further ceremony. If the teacher failed to see the upraised hand with two fingers extended and the call was urgent, the anxious party would snap the fingers or loudly call out, "Teacher! Teacher! Teacher!" to gain recognition. In those days, snapping of fingers and calling out to the teacher when necessity demanded was good form.

Some youngsters went barefoot winter and summer, and when the weather was good, a majority of the boys and some of the girls came to school unshod; so dirty feet, stone bruises, scratched and scabby feet and legs were quite an everyday occurrence.

Once in a while some young progeny would become tired and go to sleep, and on a few occasions became so relaxed, he fell to the floor with a crash, much to his chagrin and delight of the balance of the class. Mrs. Allen, being the only one who remained calm, would come to the rescue of the unfortunate sleeper.

We had no gymnasium or other play devices in the school yard and resorted to our own initiative for play and diversion. The boys and the girls each had one half of the yard to play in, and were strictly forbidden to cross over into each other's territory.

The girls played sissy games, such as one old cat, squat tag, drop the handkerchief, or ring around the rosy, black man, etc., while the boys engaged in more manly sports as leap frog, baseball, marbles, tops, and many others. The school yard in the morning, at recess, and at noon time was a milling mass of shouting, screaming, laughing, jumping, running, trick playing, and, on occasion, fighting youngsters—for all the world like a cage of monkeys.

Before the grounds were occupied by school buildings, they had been used as a cemetery on the hill towards Fitch Mountain. Tradition had it that many bodies had been overlooked, and the story was prevalent that hair, bones, teeth, and fingers had been pumped from the three wells on the school grounds. While all drank from the wells, the story would go the rounds, yet no one was made ill, and no one ever found any evidence of these wild rumors.

Mrs. Allen had taught that same grade for many years, and many of the men and women who became figures in the county's history during the past sixty years, received their first instruction in her classes for, in addition to the ABCs and the three Rs, she tried to instill in their minds and hearts respect for authority, love of school, the home, our glorious country, along with truthfulness and square dealing. She was one of those grand old teachers whose heart and soul were in her work, one whom many of the old-timers will remember with deep affection and reverence.

We had no regular lessons Friday afternoons, but devoted the time to singing, a short program, a story told or read by our dear teacher, and a spelling match, all of which was great fun.

Once a year near the end of school, she would entertain her class with a picnic, on the spacious grounds of her home. This was a great treat for kissing games were in order, and boys and girls alike entered into the sport with enthusiasm, although there were a few of both sexes too bashful to participate.

MY FIRST PRINCIPAL. At the time of entering the primary grade in 1880, Albert G. Burnett was principal of the Healdsburg Public School; he was also pastor of the Campbellite Church (now known as the Christian Church), as a side issue. Professor Burnett, as he was usually called by everyone, was a young man of fine appearance, a fluent forceful speaker, and above the average as a teacher and disciplinarian. He dressed well, always wore a black Prince Albert coat, high silk hat, and was quite some picture to look at and admire.

During recess and noon, he was always on the school grounds, just to keep an eye on the whole situation. In those far off days, there were two separate buildings and grounds for the grammar and primary schools, which were located adjacent to one another, but separated by a high board fence. To we small boys and girls of the primer class, Professor Burnett was awe inspiring, and when he came into our room on his regular tours of inspection, we sat still as mice shaking in our boots, lest he had come to punish some evil doer, but Mrs. Allen our teacher, attended to most of that with the exception of some of the large and very bad boys, in which case she would dispatch a monitor with a note to the principal, and he would come and see that proper punishment was meted out. Professor Burnett had such piercing dark eyes and looked at us so intently that we all felt sure he could read our minds, and knew our misdeeds without being told a word by any of the few tattle-tales who were always going to the teacher with their complaints.

In one of his coattail pockets he carried a leather strap, which was brought into play when occasion demanded. Punishment was usually administered before the class, or on the grounds, as a warning to others with mischievous intent. I have seen him espy an evil-doer, start on the run after the culprit and as he ran, fish the strap from his pocket

Seventh and eighth grade students wore banners representing states in this 1889 photo. They are, from left to right, as follows: (front row) Florence Southcott, Odele Enderlus, Sara King, Nellie Shipley, Violet Luedke, Olive Soules, I. Wilcox, May Raymond, Myrtle Rosenberg, Carrie Wright, Nellie Slocum, Kate Wolfe, and Lillian Hooten; (middle row) teacher Mrs. Charles Raymond, Zora Payne, Lena Zane, Florence Keene, John Flack, Maud Sarginsson, John McClish, Kate Moulton, Lizzie Ward, Mary Musen, Florence Smith, and teacher Lizzie Bonnell; (back row) Sara Marks, Mary Silvia, Florence Rose, Nora Graves, Nora Carmen, Joe Bates, Minnie Cook, Lou Seawell, and Kate Passalacqua. (Courtesy Mary Misen Cummings, Healdsburg Museum collection.)

and be ready to administer punishment the minute he collared the bad boy. On some few occasions even girls were strapped. However Professor Burnett was as able a school teacher as ever presided over a class, or applied the rod; always fair, always just, always earnest.

Later he resigned his pastorate and took up the study of law, while still acting as principal of the school and, in time, was admitted to the bar; then he resigned his position in the school department, moved to Santa Rosa to begin the practice of law and, as always, was successful. Next he ran for district attorney and was elected by a large majority. He made a fine and forceful campaign. It was in the day of political rallies, torch light processions, the firing of anvils, and large bonfires at street corners, with a great gathering in some large hall where all the party candidates sat upon the stage and were each in turn introduced by the local chairman for a few well-chosen words to the expectant and cheering throng. Attorney Albert G. Burnett was the spellbinder, and his speeches brought forth thunders of applause, and in this particular campaign he wound up his very enthralling and stimulating oration with the following climax.

He would step forward toward the audience, look them squarely in the face with his piercing dark eyes, raise his right arm high above his head with his fist clinched, extend the left hand palm up on level with his elbow, and proclaim in his very musical, penetrating as well as convincing voice, "If elected to the high office of district attorney of Sonoma County at the coming election, I promise you that I will do all within my power to see that every criminal brought before the bar of justice is incarcerated within the walls of San Quentin." At this point he would bring his right fist down into the palm of his left hand with a resounding crash to emphasize his determination to uphold the majesty of the law. This last slogan of his speech, with its spectacular finale, brought the audience to its feet with storms of applause and, of course, he was elected.

Due to his ability, energy, and popularity, his progress was ever upward. His next move was to the superior bench of the county, and then to the appellate court of the state, which position he held up to the time of his passing to his eternal reward some years ago.

Minister, teacher, attorney at law, district attorney, superior judge, justice of appellate court—Albert G. Burnett is still held in high esteem by those who knew him. He was truly an American, who, by example and precept, set the course for others to follow.

HONOR AND GLORY TO THEM ALL. Having paid a slight tribute to Mrs. Allen, my first school teacher, and A.G. Burnett, my first principal, let me now, with bowed head and due reverence, pay tribute to some other teachers who nobly played their part in shaping the character and destinies of the boys and girls who attended public school in Healdsburg in the '70s, '80s and '90s. In addition to the above named, we had Mrs. Mary McCullough, Mrs. Annie Alderson, Mrs. C.F. Raymond, Mrs. C.D. Carter, Miss Cassie Mulgrew, Miss Dessie Forseman, Miss Mollie McMannis, Miss Kate Power, Miss Nellie Brown, Miss Laura A. Varner, Miss Clara E. Heald, Miss Ruth McClelland, Miss Nannie Calhoun, and as principals the following: C.L. Ennis, J.C. Shipley (my father), and H.R. Bull.

Other teachers were a Mr. Clark, Dwight Atherton, Miss Annie O'Connor, and Miss Minnie Blake. All these gave to the job all they had, they had the welfare of the pupils at heart, and by example as well as precept they set a high standard for the classes to follow.

In looking back through the book of memory, page by page, it gives a feeling of satisfaction to recall the fact that of the approximately four hundred boys and girls who attended school at that time, very few failed in reaching the ideals set for them by their parents and teachers. In later life a few made mistakes that brought disgrace upon them but the vast majority were clean strain and true blue. To them and to their teachers all glory, honor, wisdom, and power.

A SCHOOL ROOM ACCIDENT. It must have been in the year 1885 and Mrs. Helen Raymond (wife of Charles F. Raymond) was our teacher with fifty or more boys and girls in the class and we occupied the front downstairs room in the old wooden grammar school building, long since only a memory of an older generation.

There were several large boys and girls in the class who helped make the teacher's

Mrs. Charles Raymond, one of the many teachers hailed by Dr. Shipley for "shaping . . . the characters and destinies" of Healdsburg children in the late 19th century.

life no bed of roses. Among some of these girls were Meesy Cook, Silvia Hart, and Lena Hughes; it was the latter two who, once upon a time, staged a grand fist-fight, with all rules suspended on the playground one morning, just before school took up for the day. This shocked the teacher beyond expression and delighted the kids, for while it lasted it was a cyclone of energy, as a spectacle a "honey."

The heroine of this story was Lena Hughes, a self-possessed and very husky girl who knew no fear. In those benighted days as the case may be, all girls wore homemade panties, some being made from flour sacks and held in place with one or more buttons. Once in a great while, at a critical moment, a button would give way and the none-too-dainty unmentionable or nether garment would drop to the ground or floor. If this sad accident happened to a girl when she was running on the playground her feet became hobbled and the poor unfortunate accidentee took an awful spill, which was embarrassing and sometime painful.

It was during the reading class one afternoon, when each scholar in rotation would stand in the aisle and read from the good old Appleton reader, that the following drama took place. It was Lena's turn to read a few paragraphs or until the teacher stopped her and called the next pupil. Lena was putting her whole soul into a dramatic passage and took an extra deep breath to render the climax. A button fell to the floor and rolled away without alarming her and as she swayed in giving full emphasis to her dramatic art her panties fell to the floor about her feet.

She did not faint, she did not scream in fright, she did not burst into tears of shame, for being thoroughly self-possessed and calm as a cucumber, she carefully stepped out of the trap, picked up the garment, held it high so the teacher and the class all could see and said, "Teacher, my pants fell off, can I go out and put them on." Permission was granted, the kids went into gales of laughter, Mrs. Raymond looked a bit shocked and stern, solemnly rapped for order, advised us to be more considerate of the misfortunes of others and more circumspect in our deportment.

SCHOOL DAY PRANKS. Boys and girls have been more or less the same since Cain and Abel played tag in the tall grass after Paw and Maw had been evicted from the garden of Eden, for they made faces and threw rocks at the children over in the land of Nod, to which place Cain later went, after his trouble with his brother Abel, there to take unto himself a wife or wives, and rear a large family to pester his neighbors with their pranks.

Through all ages children have romped, played, committed depredations, vexed their parents, harassed their tutors, fought, scratched, and bit one another. In fact the human race including all juveniles, with the exception of a thin veneer of so-called civilization, is today as savage as it was a hundred thousand years ago, and perhaps a little more so, for we have the benefit of the experience of past ages behind us. The boys and girls of the '80s and '90s were true to form, as full of mischief as could be, and whenever the opportunity presented, indulged in pranks that at times might have been dangerous. Some of the boys would bring mice, grasshoppers, lizards, garter-snakes, or even wild birds to school to be let loose, just for the fun of seeing the girls scream, pile on top of the desks, and hold their skirts tight about ankles, while the boys made a wild scramble to recapture the cause of the girls' alarm, each boy doing his solemn duty, and looking as innocent as the angels in Heaven.

A few times some of these same tricks were played on our dear teacher by placing one or more of the above mentioned scarecrows in her desk before school opened so when she raised her desk top to get the roll book, something would happen to tickle the kids. If the party guilty of any of these deeds was discovered he or she was fittingly punished, when the teacher failed to find the culprit all were admonished never to let that happen again, and so it went during the days of our schooling.

The men teachers would never bat an eye or wag an ear over such tricks, but some of the more frail, dainty lady teachers would throw a perfectly proper conniption fit on discovering a mouse or small snake or lizard in her desk, much to the delight of the pupils. On one April Fool occasion, Miss Laura A. Varner was our teacher, with seventy-two scholars in her room, some of the boys concocted a scheme to evacuate the room, so just before school was to take up that morning all windows were closed, an extra

The school attended by Dr. Shipley, in 1886. (Courtesy Healdsburg High School.)

stick of wood placed in the already hot stove, and as the two lines of boys and girls filed into the room from opposite doors, one of the boys managed to place a handful of cayenne pepper on the stove top.

There was a puff of smoke, and the room filled with the irritating fumes of the vaporized pepper, and how we snorted, coughed, sneezed, and cried, it was as effective as a cloud of tear gas would have been. Windows were opened to clear out the smoke, many had to leave the room, but Miss Varner being made of the staunchest of material, stood her ground, coughed, snorted, sneezed, and wiped the tears from her eyes, blew her nose, but remained master of the situation until peace, order, and comfort were restored.

Bent pins would be placed in seats for teacher to sit on, some of the boys would run pins through the tip of their shoe sole to be used as a prod to rouse some sleepy scholar. The two nebs broken from a pen and inserted in the shelf under the desk, so as to be of different length when picked with the finger gave out two rather musical notes, hard to locate, but productive of merriment. So-called spitballs would fly when our dear teacher was not looking, odd and peculiar noises produced by the inventive genius of the boys, some might study out loud just to annoy the teacher and distract the class.

Paper men, dolls, animals, and streamers would be cut out, and by a thread attached to a big soft spitball, then with the aid of a ruler heaved aloft to the ceiling, there to stick until removed; why, sometimes the ceiling of the school room would be festooned with such oddities, and when the wind blew in through the open windows they would wave and shake like leaves of an aspen tree.

Boys and girls would vie with each other trying to invent some new way of attracting attention and disrupting the calm dignity of our teachers. It would require a large volume just to record all these things alphabetically. Once some larger boys of Mrs. Allen's class in 1881 pushed little Drury Gammon (the smallest boy in the school) into an open vault half full of water, fished him out, and when he found he was still alive, all smelling like a rose, he ran into the schoolhouse to tell the teacher all about it; she, poor lady, being horrified at his sad appearance, sent him home to be cleaned up. Next day he was back at school wearing a new suit of clothes, none the worse for emersion.

ONE ON OUR TEACHER. It was about the time when our class (fourth grade) was in our early teens, perhaps 1885, that Miss Dessie Forseman was our dear teacher. She was an elder daughter of old Dr. Forseman, who had his office and residence in an ancient house on the east side of the plaza.

She had a mop of beautiful red hair, blue eyes that could snap fire when necessity demanded, had a naturally pleasing personality, was a good teacher with a burning desire for perfect lessons and deportment in her class. She took real pride in her work, rejoiced when her class responded to her able instruction, but woe betide the unlucky pupil who tried to shirk work or put anything over on her, for she saw and heard everything that went on in the room, sometimes admitting that she had eyes in the back of her head, and we almost believed her.

Of course all her dear pupils were repressed savages, and often bubbled over with a desire to have a bit of fun, or rouse her red-haired ire without getting caught, for disaster would have been the consequence.

Our class occupied the front room downstairs in the old original schoolhouse that faced on Tucker Street, and part of the day when skies were blue the gorgeous sunlight came into the room to our backs and would cast shadows on desks and floor.

It so happened that Lester Gale was my seatmate and we occupied a rear room seat on the boys' side of the school room. We were fairly good boys, both being members of Mrs. Currier's Sunday school class of the old North Methodist Church, which at that time was quite a badge of honor.

The smaller and more troublesome pupils were usually seated as near the teacher's desk as possible where she could keep her eagle eye upon them, so we must have been fairly good boys, taking all these facts into consideration.

When the event about to be related took place, Lester was turned away from me, studying his lesson diligently, the sun shone in through the open window, casting strong shadows; Miss Forseman was up in front of the girls' side dictating a lesson from Robinson's Arithmetic, a rather heavy volume. I must have been doing something of which she did not approve for she began working her way slowly and silently to the rear of the room while she kept on with her dictation until she stood directly behind my seat, her shadow falling upon the desk in front of me.

During this time I had kept a weather eye out watching her movements, for by instinct I felt sure she was after me, perhaps it was a case of guilty conscience. Without pausing in her talk to the class and having determined in her own mind I needed chastisement, she slowly raised her hand holding the book to the full length of her arm, which I observed by the shadow on my desk. As the arm and arithmetic began its descent to take me a wallop along side my dome of thought, I ducked, and as my head was not just where she expected it to be when the blow landed, she missed and gaining momentum took Lester Gale an awful crack on the side of his head behind his ear.

Not realizing that our dear teacher had made an error of judgment and thinking that I had hauled off and socked him one without warning or provocation, he turned on me in rage and right in the school room, forgetting where he was and the fact that Mrs. Currier did not allow any of her boys to use bad words, he did some rather picturesque, forceful, fluent, and extemporaneous cussing, for about two seconds the air was filled with lurid expletives.

Seeing Miss Forseman standing behind us with stark terror written on her face and realizing that it was she and not his seat mate that had almost brained him by accident, also remembering that he was in school, Lester was nonplussed and almost wilted, the class was both thrilled and horrified at the flow of profanity, our dear teacher was petrified, made speechless and for a few moments seemed aghast at the awfulness of the situation, beat it for her desk and plopped down in her chair, almost flabbergasted.

She never mentioned the incident either at that time or later for it gave her an awful scare and knocked all the props out from under her. As for myself, I was scared out of a year's growth but it was fun to have been able to put one over on our teacher, and for a long time I was a very good boy and attended to my lessons.

THE OLD ACADEMY. The original old academy was located on the east side of University Street between Tucker and Hayden; to the south of the property was the home of Mrs. Susan Currier, a Sunday school teacher; and on the east, that of Mrs. Mary McCullough, so there was a teacher on both sides, and Mrs. C.F. Raymond, another teacher, lived diagonally across the street. The old academy was well surrounded by teachers.

It was erected sometime in the '60s by a church society. If tradition and memory serves aright it was the Presbyterian, backed by a few progressive citizens. In looking through three histories of Sonoma County in my library, it is sad to find them silent on the origin and life history of this early center of higher learning.

In 1880, when I first beheld and admired this ancient structure, it occupied the center of a large lot, and was a two-story wooden building with hip roof and bell tower or cupola at its apex. In the beginning the building did have a coat of paint, but by 1880 it was weather beaten and showing the ravages of time.

The belfry was the habitation of pigeons and under the eaves were plastered many nests of mud-daubers and swallows. The bell was still in the tower and out in the yard were frames for swings and acting bars.

Originally it had been quite a school, conducted under church guidance, but like many sectarian schools that flourished in those primitive days, it had to give way to the public schools and colleges. In the year 1880 it was a vacant, decaying building where boys played after school and on Saturdays.

About this time Miss Carter and Miss Clara E. Heald came to Healdsburg, rented the building, repaired it, and started a private school known as Misses Carter & Heald

Emma Truitt (left) and Josie Cook (right) attended the "Old Academy."

Seminary, frequently referred to by some of the folks in town as the kindergarten. Shortly after opening this school, a Miss Hopkins joined the staff and for a few years it flourished, was quite popular, and then faded into the past to become only a memory.

In addition to the studies given in the public school, Miss Carter taught music and French, all three teachers instructed in good manners and dancing Friday afternoons. The whole school, excepting the little tots, occupied the large assembly hall and would go to smaller rooms for class work, so the student body was like one big family.

When school would be dismissed in the afternoon, as the long line of pupils filed out, each in turn would pause at the door, face the teacher in charge, bow gracefully, and with utmost deference, say, "Au Revoir, mademoiselle." It was a pretty ceremony and taught the girls and boys to love and respect their teachers.

Miss Carter was a lady of charm and personality. She had been to France for study and polish and was considered an excellent teacher. Miss Heald was a good teacher of a different type. She was more matter of fact, of sterner stuff, so after the seminary closed forever she taught in the public school for quite some time.

Miss Hopkins was young, very dainty, a fluffy blonde with pink cheeks and violet blue eyes, pretty as a picture and would blush to the roots of her hair, she was that shy and modest. However, she was a wonderful kindergarten teacher and all the little children loved her and would follow her about like little chickens do a hen.

As a trio they were all fine young women and had the respect and love of their students as well as the approbation of the whole community. My sister Nell and myself attended this school for one term in 1883, so the actions and events of that time are as clear as though they happened yesterday.

Many families from far out in the country, as well as those in town brought their children to this school. Many fine rigs would drive up to the entry to discharge their precious cargos and call for them in the evening. Most of the youngsters in town walked to and from school, while a few had saddle horses or ponies. Among some of the students at this temple of learning were Mamie and George Swain, Mollie McMannis, May Ruffner, May Forseman, May Redding, Emma Truitt, Josie Cook, Fannie Marks, Etta Dirvin, Sally and Blanche Hamilton, May Luedke and many others. Some of the boys were Eugene and Ellie Truitt, Frank Strong, Henry Dirvin, Grant Cook, Ben and John Grant, Ben Lathrop, and Charles Luedke. As more than fifty years have elapsed since those blissful days, many have been forgotten.

Of course in those days there was rivalry between the schools of the town, each student body thinking their school was the best and would look down on the others with disdain. The public school boys would call the boys from the advent school "Brannies," and when it came to the youngsters of the Carter and Heald Seminary, their spleen was intense, so whenever a boy from the public school met a boy from the private school the former would call out "Kindergarten eating snarten." Sometimes there would be a fist fight between contending factions, but no serious damage was done.

A modest tribute of praise for Miss Carter, Miss Heald, and Miss Hopkins, three teachers who did their very best to improve the minds, manners and morals of their charges.

P.S.: Somehow I have a faint recollection that this old building was at times spoken of as Alexander's Academy. Perhaps Cyrus Alexander had something to do with its founding.

HEALDSBURG ACADEMY. In 1877, an educator, Professor Butler, came to town and succeeded in getting the good public-spirited citizens to back his game and by public subscription they caused to be erected a rather imposing building on a large lot facing west on Fitch Street, between Matheson and Powell Streets. This school was known as the Healdsburg Academy. As there was no high school in those benighted days, this academy filled a long felt want for those who desired a bit of higher education, and for a few years was well attended and prospered.

Though built by public donations it was a private school, tuition was $5 per month for a single student and when two or more came from the same family a reasonable reduction was made, it was good business. It was by charging a tuition that the teachers were paid their salaries and the other necessary expenses of the institution were met; however, it never made a fortune.

Professor Butler was president, dean, board of directors—in fact he was the whole show and for those times had a fairly good school. Dr. Peck, a German Jew, taught history and languages. He had traveled far and wide, was called doctor as he had among many other degrees, one Ph.D. or doctor of philosophy. A Miss Mary Howard taught grammar and English. She was said to be tall, thin, rather angular, looked plain, dressed plain, was plain; but she was a past master in literature and English.

As she was brainy but not beautiful to look upon she left town when the school closed its doors still in single harness, as none of the local boys were ever interested in laying siege to her heart. Even in those primitive days the baby dolls with the "come get me" look outclassed the plain but brainy girls in the matrimonial market. For a time my father taught mathematics and bookkeeping in this school, so the academy had four average teachers who did their utmost to impart a few grains of knowledge to the minds of the then-rising generation. Most of them now are grandparents, great-grandparents, or have joined the angelic host or that of his satanic majesty in the nether regions.

As a small boy I can remember attending a graduating ceremony held in the upper rooms and of being a bit frightened at the large gathering of people, the oratory, the singing and other, to me, strange features of the glorious occasion.

Along about 1883 or '84 this school petered out and closed up shop, as it were, due to lack of attendance. It was sold to the Adventist Church in 1886 and then became the Adventist College, only to be demolished a few years later when that institution was moved to another city and the old school building and what it stood for became only a memory.

A special class composed of sixteen young men took instruction in bookkeeping and was composed of the following young bloods of the old hometown: W.W. Ferguson, Levi Appley, Ed Beeson Sr., Charles Foss, Jerry Gladden, Geo. Hudson, Arthur Mulligan, Bill Hood, Harvey Peck, George Nalley, J.W. Reynolds, George Congleton, Platt Corbelly, Frank Cummings, Ed Haigh, and Eugene Mead. In addition to bookkeeping, this class of young men took instruction in higher mathematics, and the information here supplied about them was given me by W.W. Ferguson, one of the few surviving members of that class, who has since passed away.

The academy was a co-educational institution and many of the charming members of the fair sex, including Onie Mulligan, received instructions within its walls and cheered for their alma mater. Professor Butler, in addition to being an able educator in the higher branches of learning, was quite a musician and helped the boys of his school to organize and train a band. Many of these boys later, on reaching men's estate, graduated into either the Prof. Leurch or Dr. Biddle Bands, which were eventually merged into the superlative Sotoyome Band, which made musical history in Sonoma County.

To many of the old-timers, the recollection of those happy school days will bring out of the mists of the past many pleasant memories. But like the monuments which were the wonder of the ancient world, this school, like many others in times past, has crumbled into dust.

Three: The Halcyon Days
of Childhood

THE OLD SWIMMING HOLE. It was in the glorious '80s and '90s that the boys of Healdsburg used to take themselves on foot to the old swimming hole just above the railroad bridge on Saturday afternoons and sometimes after school to disport themselves in the cool water of the Russian River. Of course these events took place in the good old summertime and the days were long and hot, and evenings perfect.

This particular swimming hole was known as Hudson's Hole, having been named after a pioneer family by the same name, who had for years lived in a big old house on the river bank just above the bridge. On the east side of the river was a fine sand bank full length of the hole, and dotted with clumps of willows, which afforded a place to undress free from observation. From the edge of this bank, the water shelved off gradually to very deep water at the opposite bank, making a perfect place to swim, dive, or paddle in the shallow water, according to the desire or ability of the bather.

Driftwood was plentiful along the banks, so many of the boys would bring a few potatoes with them, build a fire, and when the bed of coals was just right and the sand hot, the potatoes were placed and covered to be perfectly baked by the time the day's sport was ended. How good those potatoes did taste, even without butter and salt; only the palate of a healthy hungry boy can appreciate such food as manna from Heaven.

Hot dogs were almost unknown or too expensive at that time, so roast potatoes filled the bill perfectly. During green corn season, this succulent dainty was roasted by the same process with the husks left on and did those ears of sweet corn taste good? It was this method of cooking invented by our forefathers that gave the name roasting ears to green corn. Once in a while in the evenings when the boys would gather in the river in the good old summertime, they would bring a few chickens, potatoes, onions, salt, pepper, and bread and in a clean coal oil can cook up a chicken stew, while swimming, and have a feast before going to their homes and happy dreams; and were those the good old days? Occasionally some wag would tie knots in the sleeves of shirts, legs of drawers, and even sox, dipping them in water to make the knots tighter. The owners of such knotted clothing had to "chaw beef" as the saying went, for it took the combined efforts of teeth and hands to untie the knots. Sometimes this particular joke led to anger, and a few fist fights or a shower of stones thrown at the knot tiers by the boys denuded of their clothing, but as a rule the boys would forgive, forget, and be good friends after it was all over. Thus the happy days would pass.

Rafts made from old discarded railroad ties made up for the lack of boats. Some of the boys made square sails out of old sacks, and with a stick for a mast could sail with the wind as far as the riffle at the bend of the river and paddle back to repeat the sailing process. It was great fun. Of course, there were other swimming holes in the river, and one or two in Dry Creek, but the Hudson Hole above the railroad bridge was the best and most frequented by the boys as it was nearest to town.

This old swimming hole seem to be but a memory, for the channel of the river has changed since boyhood days, and many of the old landmarks have disappeared.

OUR MOTHER'S COOKIE JAR. In this day of mass production, even for cookies, doughnuts, and ginger snaps, all wrapped in cellophane and never touched by the hands of man, many of us can still remember mother's old cookie jar on the shelf behind the pantry door, with a feeling of reverence and a longing for just one of the goodies it once contained. Those old jars were of glazed pottery, some colored and fancy, others perfectly plain with lids to match and a capacity of from one to three gallons, so they varied in size. Some homes had two or three of them all in a row; one for cookies, one for doughnuts, and one for spiced pickled peaches or pears, and when the lid was removed what a pleasant aroma filled the air. It really made one's mouth water.

The cookies of those days were real cookies and the doughnuts—crisp, fragrant, and toothsome—were real homemade and fried to a beautiful brown in freshly rendered pure leaf lard, and were they good.

Occasionally a jar would be filled with some old fashioned johnnie cake made by mixing water, ground corn meal, a little white flour, mild molasses, and salt to form a thick batter, and baked rather thin in a hot oven; they were a bit dry but oh how savory; the longer you chewed them, the better they tasted. When the youngsters came home from school in the afternoon, hungry as bears, they would make a bee line for the pantry and the old cookie jar to revive their faded spirits with a handful of its delicious contents, then out into the yard or to a seat by the fire depending upon the weather, while the handful of dainties was munched in satisfaction.

Did this after-school snack spoil appetites for supper? It did not, for when the food was served for the evening meal, all came to the table with healthy hunger, hearts full of the joy of living, and did full justice to everything on the table. It may be that as we travel the sunny hillsides of life, our zest for food is dulled by the march of time, but it would seem as though the cakes, cookies, snaps, and doughnuts of our childhood, made from simple unrefined materials by our mother's hands, were far superior in every way to the modern, aseptic, vitaminized factory products with special wrappings. One thing they do lack is that element of a personal touch given by a loving mother as she prepared the things necessary for the comfort and happiness of her family.

Dr. Shipley's mother, the former Josephine Schermerhorn.

A toast to our mothers and the old cookie jars, may their memory, like a sweet fragrance, last forever.

THE SILLY SIX. Healdsburg, like all other first class metropolitan centers of the blissful '80s and '90s, had its share of gangs. Not political gangs nor criminal gangs but just plain gangs of boys and girls. Among the boys there was the Depot Buzzards, who lived near and used to romp and play about the vast depot lot, the Gas House Gang, who used to playfully cavort about Pete Dirvin's gas house as a center of activity, then there was the Sewer Rats, who lived in the north part of town and played about the Scallenger Gristmill, which was located between the main highway going north and the slough for drainage water which formed the western boundary of the then-growing town. This old mill was a little ways beyond the then-famous Kentucky saloon, and was burned to the ground in the fall of 1889.

Those gangs of boys were mostly friendly, seldom indulging in fist fights or rock throwing contests or other horseplay. But the outstanding gang of all history in the old hometown was a half dozen girls who called themselves the Silly Six. This was way back in the days before a high school had been started, when many of the subjects now taught in such temples of learning were part of the course of study in the first or the highest grade of the grammar school, and many of the upper class students were in their early twenties.

This gang of girls ranged in age from eighteen to twenty years and were as full of giggles, squeals, squirms, laughter, and energy as a dog is full of fleas. They flocked together like a bunch of blackbirds, where every one went the rest would follow; they were inseparable morning, noon, and night, it was a wonder if they even went to their own separate homes to sleep. They saw fun and frolic in everything that happened, something was always sure to tickle them and as they were squealing, giggling, or laughing most of the time they were well named.

These six girls were from the finest old families in the town, were all good lookers, in fact some were outstanding beauties and if they were transplanted into the present day no doubt they would all be in the movies for they had what it takes and the personal qualifications for movie queens. They liked the boys and the boys were wild over them. Many of the old hardshell, diehard mossbacks looked at the Silly Six with dubious expression and would shake their knowing heads in disapproval of their antics; however, nearly all these girls married fine men, settled down, and became good wives and mothers.

No doubt all old-timers will recall this conspicuous covy of giddy, giggling girls, for in their day they were the leading feature and the talk of the town. Some would praise, others would condemn, the younger boys looked up to them and adored, the boys of their own age or a bit older were flattered to serve them, their popularity with this last class was unbounded, this contingent of the male population were their abject slaves and would gladly follow when ever called.

Father Time, that leveler and tamer of all things human and inhuman, has no doubt converted those who survive of the Silly Six into staid, decorous old ladies for half a century is a lot of time. It is a pleasure to call them to mind, for in their day they were unique, celebrated, and beautiful; I know, for if one of them chanced to speak to me, a runt of a boy, I was raised to the seventh heaven of ecstatic joy.

HUNTING BIRD EGGS. Again we follow the winding path down memories lane back to the days of our youth before it was unlawful to gather birds' eggs and do a lot of other things which are now forbidden or otherwise out of date in this fast-moving world of ours, controlled by the sobsisters, the jayhawkers, along with all the crazy array of alphabetic bureaus and other tripe.

In the '80s and '90s most of the boys were ardent collectors of birds' nests and eggs, which at that time was considered commendable and perfectly proper as it showed an interest in natural history and kept the boys out of other mischief, out in the open which was good for their health.

During the mating season of the birds many of the boys were out in the fields, along the streams and through the woods in quest of new and rare specimens of the marvelous handiwork and energy of our feathered friends. Many birds at that time were considered enemies of man, especially the English sparrows who built their nests about the houses and made a lot of noise.

The boys would hunt singly, in pairs, or by threes or fours and great was the rivalry as to who could find the most nests as well as the greatest variety. Some of the boys would sell sets of nests with a full complement of eggs to be placed in public museums, which was part of the game for it brought in quite a bit of small change which helped us get things we really needed.

It was lots of fun to wander carefree, far and wide, intently scanning every bush, tree, clump of grass, or tule patch, for the birds had a way of hiding their nests in the most unlikely places and great was the joy when our efforts were rewarded. Of course a nest full of young birds or a setting of eggs that were about to hatch were never molested, for there was even in those glorious days honor among thieves.

Our collections contained the nests and eggs of humming birds, wild canaries, linnets, finches, sparrows, blue birds, pee-wees, thrushes, robins, brown birds, black birds, orioles, larks, doves, quail, beemartins, roadrunners, swallows or mud daubers, blue jays, woodpeckers, yellow-hammers, owls, hawks, crows, mud hens, kildees, and many others we were unable to name or classify. The rarer they were and the harder to get, the greater the prize with bubbling joy in proportion.

When out hunting we always shared alike, the finder of the nest having first choice of eggs as they varied in color and beauty even in the same nest for nature seldom produces two things exactly alike. While in quest of birds' eggs many amusing things would happen to add a bit of spice to our young lives.

Sometimes a nest of eggs would be lowered from a tall tree in a hat to which a ball of twine had been attached or by some other safe and sane method, but occasionally when the nest was in a hollow tree high up from the ground, no hat being handy, the eggs would be brought down in the boy's mouth to prevent breakage.

Once Bert Soules, Lydon Shaw, Dellie Hassett, and myself had located a woodpecker

Ed Green tried his raccoon hunting skills near the McClish Ranch on Westside Road. (Courtesy Paul Ragghianti, Healdsburg Museum collection.)

nest in a tall dead tree, so the best climber of the quartet shinnied up the tree with a small hatchet tucked in the strap at the back of his pants so as to chop out the nest if it contained eggs. On reaching the nest he scared the mother bird away and found four beautiful eggs so the opening was enlarged, the hatchet dropped, the eggs removed, and carefully placed in his mouth for a perfectly safe descent.

In his hurry and elation he had failed to notice that the eggs were about to hatch, which was a grave error. In climbing down the tree he received several jolts and on reaching the ground felt a squirming in his mouth and spat out four newly hatched woodpeckers together with the scraps of shell which had housed the little birds. Of course the rest of us had a hearty laugh at the boy who had hatched the young birds in his mouth, but he could not see the fun for he did a lot of spitting, complaining that there was a very peculiar taste in his mouth which he proceeded to wash out with good old Russian River water. And so the round of life went on with its ups and downs, skinned shins, torn clothes, with an occasional trouncing at home for some real or fancy depredation.

THOSE OLD SWEETHEARTS OF OURS. Turning back the pages of the book of memory to the days of our budding youth, when life was just one sweet dream after another, we see in fancies' mirror the many beautiful faces of those old sweethearts of ours.

Sometimes we wonder what has become of them, are they living or are they dead, if alive, what do they look like today, would they have the same overpowering appeal as they did when we were just school kids taking our first unsteady steps on the broad pathway of life with all its vicissitudes and adventures.

Most of the boys of the '80s and '90s at one time or another had their sweethearts, sometimes they were a bit older, sometimes a little younger, some even fell in love with their teachers, especially if they were young and good looking, for when the fire of young love burns brightly, age, station, religion, or race make little difference.

Young love must have its flare, burn fiercely for a time and die, only to be rekindled by some new charmer. It was seldom that a boy got through his schooldays without being badly stung by the love bug. Some got stung so often and recovered so quickly that they averaged a new girl every month in the year, while others only once or twice a year, although a few there were who disliked the girls and never fell victim to the venom of the aforementioned insect.

What happened to them later in life is unknown, some may still be woman haters, but the majority no doubt became dignified heads of happy families. A few of the boys were more constant and only changed sweethearts at rare intervals, but the majority were on again, off again, gone again with amazing rapidity. How this on and off adoration affected the girls there is no means of knowing as a little time heals all wounds. Some were boy shy, even boy haters, the majority were willing to be admired, and still others were out and out huntresses, like Diana, only they confined their activities to the boys instead of the denizens of the forests.

The girl that caught my fancy during my first month of school was a very pretty black-eyed French girl, Amanda DeMuse. She was a picture, and as dainty as a flower, was in the seventh or the next higher grade, and Mrs. McCullough was her teacher. Once each month on a Friday afternoon Mrs. Allen's class would march into Mrs. McCullough's room for a combined singing and literary program which was great fun.

Our class would take seats on benches all around the room just under the blackboards and fill up such vacant seats as were available, some even sitting three in a seat. On this first visit to the higher grade, as we marched in, I noticed that Amanda was occupying a rear seat all by herself, so in ignorance of the rules and throwing all caution to the winds, I allowed my admiration of this baby doll to get the better of what little sense I had left, and I sat down in the seat with her, so as to be near this youthful idol, where I might admire in silence for I knew whispering was not permitted. Well, as I sat down a scared look came over her face, and she went out into the next aisle, frantically waving her hand and snapping her fingers.

Mrs. McCullough saw, realized the gravity of the situation, and came to the rescue of the maiden in distress. I was escorted to the sidelines and seated on a bench at the same time being admonished that boys and girls could not sit together. Of course I was crestfallen and felt like a half-penny for displaying such simple ignorance, but before long found another girl to look at and admire, one who was not so shy.

Some of the other boys had equally harrowing experiences in different ways. However we all lived to find new sweethearts, many times, before our school days ended. The DeMuse family, consisting of a father, mother, two pretty daughters, and a son who was in my class, moved from Healdsburg the next year and were lost forever.

In the words of Bobby Burns, "Can old acquaintance be forgot," etc. Then here's to those old sweethearts of ours, both living and gone to a better world; may their memory ever bloom like the rose fresh with morning dew, beautiful, fragrant, eternal.

SEEING NELLIE HOME. *"In the sky the bright stars glittered, On the banks the pale moon shone, It was from Aunt Dinah's quilting party, I was seeing Nellie home."* How the words of that beautiful old song bring back memories of that period in our lives when in our teens, just as the down first began to grow on cheek, chin, and upper lip, we thrilled at the prospect of seeing some pretty girl home from a party, a social, or from evening church services.

Most of the boys and girls of that era had been told ghost stories by their grandmothers and as a result were afraid of the dark, excepting when two or more were together, for no apparition, no matter how blood-thirsty, ever attacked when two was company or three a crowd. Also, there were two or three old unoccupied houses in town said to be haunted, and young folks always gave them a wide berth after dark, except when in mass formation.

So it happened that at the age mentioned when boys began to see the girls home, we would screw up our courage and ask the lady of our choice if we could have the pleasure of seeing her home, and if accepted, our hearts almost skipped a beat, our joy was unbounded, we were way up in the clouds, so to speak, or walking on air instead of terra-firma.

"On my arm her soft hand rested, Rested light as ocean foam."

And so, whether it be from a party, social, or divine services in the evening or in our later teens, from a dance, Nellie took the proferred arm, daintily, timidly, so beautifully described in the above two lines of quotation, and with a feeling of pride in possession we would proudly march off to the lady's home, taking as long as possible to make the trip, "for the longest way round is the sweetest way home."

Occasionally Nellie might have other plans or have tired of our saphead dignity and would decline the offer of escort for some other fellow, in which case the depths of despair were ours, for if the other boys happened to see the snub that particular boy was in for a razzing. As many boys were afraid of the dark, they would frequently team up and ask girls who lived not too far apart so as to meet and keep each other company on the return journey.

Of course no boy at the time would come right out and admit that he was afraid of the dark but where two were together it gave confidence and they had no fear of ghosts. When the girl had no near neighbor and lived quite a ways that was very different, especially on dark or stormy nights, for there were no street lights in those halcyon days in Healdsburg and the boy had to make the trip home with utmost speed in darkness and terror.

For my own part (after the passage of some fifty years) I will admit of being afraid of the dark at that time, so when it became necessary to go places at night, especially after seeing Nellie home, the middle of the road was the most comfortable place and to

The Healdsburg Plaza was still a fairly undeveloped area in 1872, the year Dr. Shipley was born. Wagons used the plaza as a parking lot. (Joseph H. Downing photograph.)

whistle some of these grand old hymns like "Rock of Ages," "Nearer My God to Thee," or the like, gave a feeling of confidence and security—at least I would have the Lord on my side if the devil and his imps did show up, or a ghost or hobgoblin crossed my path.

No one was ever molested but some of the boys including myself had some awful hair-raising frights, at fancied moving shadows, the groaning of a tree limb against its fellow, the hoot of an owl, or a cat or dog suddenly running across the path.

My what a relief it was to get home with a whole skin, where all was safe; then we could go to bed and dream of that exquisite pleasure of seeing Nellie home.

THE GRAVEYARD GHOST. It was in the good old summertime, perhaps in the late '70s, long before the boys of my own age were old enough or had the bravery to take a girl out for a walk in the moonlight, so any and all of them are hereby eliminated.

At the time this ghost made his appearance the party who saw it must have been about twenty-five years old, was the town's beau brummel, some folks called him a fop. He dressed well, looked well, carried a malacca cane, thought himself about the proper caper, and was considered a lady killer, i.e. he admitted that he had a way with the fair sex and that no lady could long resist his charms.

One might say that he was conceited, suffering from an exaggerated ego. We have all met such beings in this world of ours. I have heard my mother's uncle, S.H. Wood, who lived on Tucker Street, tell the story and go into gales of laughter until tears ran down his cheeks, even telling who the party was, so it must be true.

It was the custom in those days of ignorant simplicity for young lovers to stroll in the moonlight, here, there and elsewhere. Seaman's Pasture adjacent the Oak Mound Cemetery was a favorite place for lovers to frequent for there were some logs and fallen trees where they could sit and spoon and goo at one another, as lovers sometimes do.

During the day many locally owned cows were pastured in the large enclosure; occasionally a dry cow or a calf might be left there overnight. On this particular night the couple, consisting of the local Adonis and one of Healdsburg's more gorgeous young ladies, had wandered to a spot near the entrance gate of the cemetery and were seated on a log. Our hero was dilating in words of fire upon the fierceness of his love—you all know that kind of bull a boastful swain can throw in an effort to impress as well as delude some fair maiden.

Well they had been there for perhaps an hour, enjoying the night, the moon, and the stars and he had told her over and over again of his great and burning love, which would last 'til time should be no more; in fact, for her sake he could vanquish a dragon, as did the knights of old for love of a fair maiden.

While thus delightfully engaged a white calf strayed quietly up behind from the direction of the graveyard. No doubt the calf was lonesome and desired human company for it put its cold nose up against his neck behind the ear, blew a lung full of hot breath, and at the same time gave him a lap with its tongue.

The fastidious young gentleman must have used "New Mown Hay" as perfumery for the calf seemed to like him. No man, no matter how brave, could withstand such a shock, and catching a glimpse of the white apparition over his shoulder he leaped into the air with a blood-curdling scream and landed on his feet on the dead run with the calf after him. His shrieks penetrated the still night air as he out distanced the calf, cleared the pasture fence with a single bound and beat it for the hotel where he lived, entirely forgetting the girl, his love, and his bravery.

To make a sad story sadder, the young lady, after her first scare, realizing it was only a calf, calmed her fears and bravely set out for home all by her lonely, realizing the frailty of men and vowing vengeance for her untimely desertion. Next day she sent a rather caustic note to the hero of this story, informing him that she never wanted to see him again and for him never to call on her again.

Of course the story got around and the other boys who were a bit jealous of the dandy twitted him so much that he left for other parts not being a regular Healdsburger. The beautiful lady married a less flashy man and lived happily ever after.

OUR MOTHER'S MEDICINE. The old saying that "Little pitchers have big ears" contains a lot of truth in more ways than one, for way back in the days as a small boy I used to listen in when neighbor ladies told my mother about some of the wonderful medicines they used to cure their families of aches, pains, and other ills.

In those days money was scarce and the solemn visaged, bewhiskered doctor was only called in when some dire calamity or serious illness befell the family. Minor troubles, cuts, bruises, and the diseases of childhood were cared for by our devoted mothers or by some wrinkled, toothless old lady, versed in roots and "yarb," so they developed a homemade medical practice all their own, which had been handed down with modifications, generation after generation from time immemorial.

I can remember well how carefully my mother would study "Dr. Gunn's Family Doctor," a very large book full of good old-fashioned common sense advice to mothers for the care of themselves, their husbands, and children; so that she would be better able to cope with our measles, mumps, chickenpox, spells of croup, coughs, colds, etc. and how to pull our first or so-called milk teeth with a linen thread.

It may be that this grand old family standby had something to do with my choice of medicine as a life work, for before I could read I used to look at the pictures in it and wonder, later on reading many chapters and marveling at their words of wisdom. Anyway, it was the work of a master mind to help our mothers through a trying period, the rearing of a family under primitive conditions.

Fifty or more years ago when heat was to be applied to make a child sweat, it would be rolled up in a blanket and rung from hot water and hot bricks or stove lids, or ears of field corn boiled in water would be applied outside the blanket. It was a bit uncomfortable but very effective.

Bran or mush poultices along with flaxseed and slippery elm bark were in use for local inflammations, as was that ancient and time-honored medicament, the fresh "cow-flop" poultice, which is still in use in many parts of the world and has a great reputation.

To make measles or other eruptive diseases break out well, some gave hot "nanny berry" tea. The berries were gathered from the sheep fold. To cure croup a child might be given a teaspoonful of its own urine, which was considered a sure cure. One might say these methods were an early form of organic medicine, for some of these same things are being used today, only in a more refined form and distinguished with gigantic names.

Boneset, sage, camomile, fennel, and many other garden plants were used in the form of tea for diverse and sundry ills. Salt, black pepper, and vinegar were used as a mouth wash and gargle—it must have been potent for it had an awful taste—and pumpkin seeds for worms along with castor oil and turpentine to clinch the cure.

As a blood medicine and spring tonic, brimstone, cream of tartar, and treacle were a routine treatment for young and old. It was a good medicine then and is today, if you like it. Onion syrup was a tower of strength for coughs and colds in many homes, an effective medicine but "heck" to take. Soap with brown sugar as well as fat pork was used for many external troubles, including boils, carbuncles, and felons. If they did no good they caused no harm.

For cuts, bruises, and other abrasions of the skin, axle grease from the wheel of a wagon was a favorite and effective remedy. Hot water bottles were unknown in those days but if we go way back to the time of David, the sweet singer of Israel, we find the application of external heat mentioned in the Bible. In First Kings, first chapter, and first verse, we read, "Now King David was old and stricken in years, and they covered him with clothes, but he got no heat."

So, as beautifully described in the few following verses they got a fair damsel, whose blood was warm, to get in bed with the old boy and snuggle up close to the poor old king to keep him warm, and evidently the medicine worked. You may read it yourself. You see, there is nothing new under the sun.

Many other home remedies were in use, among them angleworm oil, skunk oil, "bar's" goose grease, and mutton tallow along with a lot of others, long since forgotten. With all our modern progress we find there is a trace of common sense in ancient medicine as there is today along with a whole lot of bunk and hooey.

To our mothers we owe an undying debt of gratitude, for they did a good job of doctoring our ills; they nursed us at their breasts instead of feeding us a formula or some patent provender from a can or antiseptic package. They rocked us to sleep in their loving arms or they crooned a lullaby, and did not slop cocktail dregs on our bibs or drop cigarette ashes into our innocent baby eyes.

To them—their primitive medicines—and their simple ways, our ever-lasting praise and reverence.

YOUTHFUL ANGLERS. Way back yonder in the days of our youth when, from sun to sun, and back again to the next sun, life was more or less a round of joy, except when we had to stay after school or we received a good sound trouncing at the hands of our devoted parents, who were trying to bring us up in the way that we should go, fishing with rather crude tackle was one of the pastimes many of the small boys enthusiastically enjoyed.

Most boys' fishing tackle in those simple days consisted of willow poles, cane poles, or, rarely, bass wood jointed rods with lace wood tip given as a premium by the *Youth's Companion* for securing a new subscriber. Their lines and hooks were of the simplest material, some even using heavy linen thread and a bent pin, nothing like the gaudy lures and expensive tackle of our present day.

The boys used to fish for trout in all the streams about Healdsburg from Sausal Creek, Warm Springs Creek, Peña Creek, Mill Creek, and even as far as Austin Creek, and what loads of trout we usually would catch! Some mighty fine ones along with the small fry as in those days there was no limit as to size of fish or catch.

When water was fairly high in Russian River and Dry Creek, fishing for suckers, hardmouth, and perch with pole or line or with throw lines, which might be left overnight at times, produced some mighty fine fish; occasionally a salmon might be taken in this way. Some of the older boys would go out gigging for salmon when the run was on and what heroes they were to we small boys, especially when they came back through town with a beautiful silver side dangling from the gig over their shoulder; and how they would strut as they passed disdainfully by the runts of boys.

Probably the most fun was derived from fishing in the old slough, part of which ran through town near Sing Lee's laundry and the celebrated Kentucky Saloon and the western edge of town, emptying itself into Dry Creek after passing through the ranch lands of Charles Alexander, Albert Bell, my father, J.H. Curtiss, the Redding, Amesbury and the W.N. Gladden ranches. Trout, chubs, hardmouths, perch, minnows, and other small fish—even sticklebacks —would be taken in abundance when the slough was full of water and running freely. Near the home of Uncle Chas. Alexander, close to the spot

The Shipley home in Cloverdale.

where the railroad track crosses the 101 Highway and Dry Creek Road, was a deep hole known to all small boys as Alexander's Hole. Some days when skies were clear and the fishing good, thirty or forty boys of various ages would be evenly spaced about this body of water after school or on Saturdays, each industriously engaged in seeing how many fish he could take from its rily depths. Friday and Beany Cook (brothers), Harry Emerson, Walter Conner, Measy Cook, Coonie Soules, Jindee Shaw, Dellie Hassett, Frank Gum, the Haigh boys, Bert and Rainey, Sealskin Miller, Dutchy Fried, Spoonie Vaughan, Lester Gale, Jake and Henry Stussy, Gene and Ellie Truitt, Charley Dodge, and many others including this narrator enjoyed the privilege of following the example of Isaac Walton in this spot. And what fun we had, especially if one of the boys happened to lose his footing and went kerplunk into the cold muddy water. It was great fun for the rest of the little savages, but woe to the poor kid who received the ducking, for a warm reception usually awaited him on his return home.

Before my days as a fisherman, when I was too small to be allowed far from home, I once saw a sturgeon that was caught by my great uncle, S.B. Wood, in the same slough just back of the Sotoyome Hotel. If memory serves me correctly, this fish was about three feet long, although at the time it appeared to me to be as large as a whale.

In those days there were a few sturgeon in Russian River and its tributaries, but at present the species seems to be extinct. On one occasion Sterling Nourse, Lydon Shaw,

Bert Soules, Dellie Hassett, and myself went on a day's fishing trip out to Mill Creek. We started at four in the morning on an April 1, on foot with our lunches, cane poles, and gunny sacks for creels, necessity being the mother of economy, for there was no money for fanciful tackle or equipment.

We tramped all the way out to the Old Mill, baited our hooks, and started bobbing for fish. We all used cork floats and lead sinkers so when the fish deep down on the water took the hook, the cork on the surface would warn us by bobbing up and down. The only thing we caught was a few chubs, some water dogs, and one turtle. As the morning was cloudy, and having no watches with which to tell time, when our stomachs told us we were hungry we proceeded to devour our lunches, and having caught all the fish we did not want, and having taken no trout and being a bit disgusted with our luck, we traced our steps homeward, arriving just before noon—so we all proceeded to eat another meal. Some of the other boys of this story may recall this little event as an outstanding fishing trip in the days of our youth.

LOCAL SPITFIRE. Way back in the mid-'80s, there lived, in the old hometown, a rather outstanding girl the boys called "Spitfire." She had as peppery a temper and as sarcastic and fluent a tongue as any female of the species since the days of Zantipe, the shrewish wife of poor old Socrates.

If any of the boys wanted a bit of fun or wished to start a verbal cyclone all they had to do was cross her path, make an ugly face, poke a finger or stick at her, or merely say "spitfire" and the riot was on in full fury. She would even scrap with the other girls in the school yard or on the way to and from school, but her special hatred was the pestiferous boys. Her temper was set to a hair trigger and sometimes it went off automatically. Otherwise she was a perfectly normal girl.

One day Ellie Truitt, Charley Dodge, and several other boys of about their age got her cornered in front of Truitt's Theatre on Center Street and proceeded to annoy her with remarks, grimaces, and gestures intended to arouse her ire. Well, this worked differently for, seeing that she was treed, so to speak, she became silent, backed into a corner to protect her rear and flanks, and while she looked daggers, her black eyes ablaze, she kept her lips tight shut but worked her mouth from side to side, up and down, in and out, vigorously for several minutes while all the time the semi-circle of teasing boys closed in nearer.

When she was all ready with a mouthful of saliva and the boys were within easy range and off-guard, she let drive all she had full in their faces. This barrage was unexpected and overwhelming, so, while the boys were engaged in clearing their vision, coughing, spitting, and wiping their countenances, she gave several of them a few vigorous rights and lefts to their jaws and made good her escape while they were busily engaged and temporarily confused.

It was a great battle, one girl against several boys and the girl, due to her quick strategy, came off victor. After that episode when any of the boys wanted to tease her they did it at a safe and respectful distance. If memory serves me correctly the girl's name was Florence and her folks lived on Center Street.

The old town has produced its share of celebrities, artists, musicians, champions in sports, and other lines—even famous beauties, but it produced only one Spitfire.

GLAMOUR GIRLS. Looking back through the thickening gloom of bygone years to that bright spot in our lives which was our school days, in fancy's mirror we can trace the beautiful faces, charms, manners, and the usual personalities of the girls we used to admire. Healdsburg had more than its share and then some of outstanding girls from every point of view—brains, ability, good looks, and "umph!" Some enjoyed a widespread popularity, others were admired by a few, and perchance a very small number had but one admirer.

Some were given oral acclaim and were stars of the first magnitude, others received a deep and abiding admiration in a quieter way, while a very few were worshiped in silence, for vim, vigor, vitality, volubility, veracity, vehemence, and viscosity these girls had no peers; only a few can be mentioned in a sketch of this character.

There was Ann O'Connor, an exquisitely beautiful brunette, who taught school for a number of years and who later became Mrs. Wood Wattles. She was an all-round girl—quite a singer and elocutionist, who appeared many times in local amateur entertainments.

Then we had the three Emerson girls, Nellie, Millie, and Mamie. The last was in my class in school. They were all good lookers, fine girls in every sense of the word, and will always be remembered by old-time Healdsburgers.

Then there was that transcendentally beautiful and charming girl, May Redding, whose nickname was Pidge, over whom the boys were daffy. Another girl whom the boys used to admire was Etta Watson, nicknamed "Waxie," so called by the boys because she was a beautiful blue-eyed blond with a peaches and cream complexion that gave the impression that she must have been molded of wax. She needed no artificial make-up, it would have spoiled her natural beauty.

Along in the late '80s, a girl came to school and immediately created a furor. The boys all went wild over her. She was Irish, good-looking, full of fire with a quick come-back and could out-do them all with her witty tongue. Her name was Carrie Dougherty. When first asked what her name was she told the guys it was Bridget Baloney and it stuck from that time on and that's what everyone called her. She was a good scrapper either verbally or physically and how the boys did hang on her words.

Speaking of blondes calls to mind that stately, graceful, serene young lady, Pearl Cottle. She was an ash blonde with a head of hair that would make a braid as big as your arm and hung well below her waist. She was adored in silence by many of the boys.

There was another teacher, Nellie Brown, who possessed wit, fire, charm, and an indomitable spirit. She was a general favorite. To name one by one all the girls of those halcyon days who would come into this category would take reams of paper, but to those old-timers who are still here and can remember, just put on your thinking caps and look for yourselves, recalling those glamour girls of long ago.

NOTE. None of the aforementioned glamour girls were on my list of school-day sweethearts. The memories of *them* are locked within the treasure chest of dreams.

Four: Entertainment, Social Groups, and Celebrations

The Healdsburg Cadets. It was about the middle of the '80s that some members of the GAR organized the Healdsburg Cadets, a semi-military social club for boys from twelve years of age up. We had some fifty or sixty members ranging from four to six feet tall, all were of school age and attended the Healdsburg public school, there being no high school in those primitive days.

Our instructor was a Mr. Logan, a veteran of the Civil War, a GAR leader and the owner of a shoe store and a cobbler shop on the east side of the plaza. We drilled in the school yard when the weather was fine, and in Nosler's Hall during the winter months. We all took a great pride in our drills and could do "fours right or left," "fours on into line," or "fours right or left into line," and different facings with the precision of veterans, and of course had to have some kind of uniforms, as we were to appear in the Fourth of July parade and wanted to put on a lot of dog.

Having little money among the whole company, we purchased some second-hand uniforms from a marching club in San Francisco. They consisted of white canvas jacket trimmed in red cotton braid, with crossed cannons made from red oil cloth, white duck leggins also trimmed with red. Some of these uniforms had to be cut down to fit smaller boys and some were dirty and had to be washed, which caused the red dye to run, giving a pink appearance to the white duck, but they were uniforms, and we felt all puffed up and real swell.

We had a captain, a first and second lieutenant, an orderly sergeant, a few corporals, and were full-fledged military company without arms. We had a drum corps of four drums, and how the drummer boys would ply the sticks and make the echoes ring with martial sounds. Collie Gum, George Warfield, Harry Logan, Woodberry Goodwin, Lewis Stewart, and a few other large boys were officers and leaders in the organization. Once each year we had an annual feed and a bowl of Tom and Jerry, which was a great event. With our grandeur and our beautiful second-hand uniforms we did our best to make an impression and thrill the girls, for a soldier boy was something to be proud of in those halcyon days.

Like all temporal things the Healdsburg Cadets had a glorious beginning, a transcendent rise, and after a few years an inglorious end, for like a dry barrel in the summer when the hoops are removed, it fell to pieces and passed into history.

THE YELLOW JACKETS. It was in those easy going days of Healdsburg's primitive glory that whole swarms of yellow jackets would occasionally on Saturday afternoon, Sundays, or on holidays come buzzing into town to have a good time and admire the pretty girls. These insects were not of the genus (vespa maculata) and had no definite sting—they were boys and young men, nice fellows all.

They were called Yellow Jackets by many of the local folks, especially the young bloods of the town, because they wore gray uniforms elaborately ornamented with gold braid, brass buttons, natty caps with plenty of gold braid, and a yellow plume standing up in front like an exclamation point; all this splendor made a gorgeous picture either singly or enmasse.

These Yellow Jackets were students at the Litton Springs Military Academy, some three miles north of town where the Salvation Army Home is now located.

As a military body they were cavalry dismounted, so when on parade they wore in addition to their brilliant uniforms huge sabers of Civil War period. For some of the smaller boys these mighty weapons were quite a load to pack and almost dragged on the ground.

This very popular military academy was conducted by a Professor Gamble as head master or proctor, with a Major Shakespere (a West Point graduate) as instructor in mathematics and military tactics and technique. There was one other teacher whose name is forgotten. This school was considered quite high class and many boys and young men attended, especially from well-to-do families about the bay.

Some of these bloods were a bit hard for their dear parents to manage so they were sent to this socially correct military school where they could receive instruction in the arts and sciences as well as discipline at one and the same time.

At Fourth of July parades and other outstanding events the Yellow Jackets, under command of Major Shakespere, would participate, evolute, and go through the manual of arms for the saber, all of which made some of the local boys green with envy, for the big girls and charming young ladies were sure to be impressed and fall for the boys in those blindingly brilliant uniforms, as they were, so to speak, swept off their feet.

If memory serves me right, out in front of the main building at the academy was located a tall flag pole and nearby stood an old-fashioned gun of about three-inch bore which was fired at sunrise and sunset, when Old Glory was raised in the morning and lowered from the staff at retreat with the troop drawn up in perfect formation and standing at attention, saluting.

It has been so many years since this celebrated school crumbled into the dust, figuratively speaking, that most of the boys who attended have been forgotten, but memory is still clear on one—Charles Litton, a cousin of the Haigh boys and a lineal descendant of the original owners and discoverers of the mineral springs that bear the family name.

Chas. Litton was a fine looking young man and when he came to visit with the Haigh boys all decked out in his uniform on a Saturday afternoon it gave the boys of the neighborhood a great thrill to gather in the Geo. Haigh backyard, corner of East and Hayden Streets, and with mouths and eyes wide open gaze in wonder and admiration at the Haigh boys' marvelous cousin and if he allowed us to play ball with him our joy was unbounded.

Charles Litton was a fine fellow; later he became a dentist and for many years has followed his profession in the city of Stockton. Time and tide waits for no man, the onward rush of modern life has blotted out many educational institutions in the old hometown that for a time served the community; the old Alexander Academy, the Healdsburg Academy, the Carter and Healds Seminary, the Litton Springs Military Academy, and the Adventist Academy, and even before these there were two very small private schools before the sixties.

THE BATTLE OF THE BANDS. In the '80s Healdsburg was noted for the number and quality of its musicians of all kinds, vocal and instrumental. Professor Leurch (spelling uncertain but pronounced Lurch) was one of the outstanding music teachers, and leader of Leurch's brass band, which was famous in the county for the quality of its music and the beauty of its uniforms.

The uniforms were navy blue, trimmed with plenty of red and gold braid, their helmets were topped with red plumes, and, with polished horns, the ensemble was magnificent. The drum major was tall, wore a gigantic bearskin hat, and with his gold balled baton, ornamented with red silk cords and tassels, was thrilling—and how he could strut his stuff, twirl, gyrate, and toss that baton. The boys would cheer as he drew near, and the girls would say, "ain't he sweet." It was some band of thirty-odd pieces, and Healdsburg was justly proud of it.

There were a lot of other good tooters in town, not members of the Leurch Band, and so Dr. Biddle, a dentist and musician, organized the Biddle's Silver Cornet Band as opposition. The new band had light blue uniforms, trimmed with white and gold, and their helmets were set off with snow white plumes. All their instruments were silver-plated, numbering thirty-six pieces. They sure could play, and created some sensation. Their drum major was gorgeous in light blue, white and gold braid, with all the other trappings, and of course they tried to put it all over the rival band.

As a result of this rivalry, a bit of jealousy sprang up between them, each having their following who took sides, while the larger percentage of people remained neutral, admired and praised both bands, for nothing in the county could equal them in appearance or musical ability. Soon the opposing factions did not like each other, and would sling verbal mud at each other, individually and collectively, and the tension grew, but no blood was ever shed. When one band was playing, the other would remain silent and scowl, and visa versa. At times they even refused to appear in the same parade together, and when they did, it was evident from the sidelines that each had a vigorous contempt for each other.

Around 1884, the Sotoyome Band included the following, from left to right: (front row) J.W. Gladden, D.O. Davis, George E. Bailhache, Charles Grant, and "Pop" Dolky; (back row) Ed Fenno, W.W. Ferguson, J.T. Bailhache, John Hickey, Charles H. Butler, drum major L.A. Norton, J. Falvy, Joe McDonough, Fred Bailhache, Millard Hall, and Charles B. Proctor. (Courtesy Ethel Reiners, Healdsburg Museum collection.)

The Town Band (in the foreground) and the Pastime Minstrels (behind them) gathered in front of Truitt's Opera House on Center Street, c. 1910. (Courtesy Vivian Hall, Healdsburg Museum collection.)

This state of undercover war went on for about two years, when through the influence of mutual admirers who were members of a committee for a grand Fourth of July celebration, the two bands and their leaders were made to see the error of their way, bury the hatchet, and become friends again, so on this grand and glorious occasion they headed the parade in mass formation, alternating the men of each band, headed by the two drum majors, and the town went wild with delight, the event was a success and everybody was made happy.

Changing times and personnel brought changes in the bands, and from the two the Sotoyome Band was evolved under the leadership of Professor D.C. Smith, which band for years was well and favorably known far and wide. "Sic transit gloria mundi."

THE CHILDREN OF ISRAEL. Going back into the dawn of Healdsburg's history we find that, along with other races and creeds who settled in the trading post bearing the name of that hardy old pioneer Harmon Heald, came some of the chosen people. Jacob Mitchell being among the first and not long after than in the '60s and '70s came that grand old man (then in his budding youth and vigor) Wolf Rosenberg, of whom we will speak later. There were Jonas Bloom and Samuel Cohen, who were in the general merchandise business and owned a warehouse by the railroad track across the river; later this property was purchased by the Van Allen brothers and converted into the first fruit cannery in town. Sam Meyer owned and operated a great store on West Street and advertised to the world that he carried everything. Marks Meyer, a relative of Sam's, was in the wool, hide, and junk business with a warehouse on Center Street, south of Nosler's Hall. The Goldstein family had a gent's furnishing store on West Street, between the Union Hotel and the Riley & Fox Drug Store, then known as the Red Front Drug Store, because the front of the ancient brick building had been painted a vivid red.

All these men with the exception of Jonas Bloom had families and goodly numbers of sons and daughters who attended school with the rest of us. We were all good friends and got along fine together, in spite of heedless razzing by some thoughtless gentile children. Jonas Bloom was a bachelor, quite a dandy, dressed well, drove a fine horse and buggy, and was some beau with many of the gentile young ladies, who were delighted to go out with him, for he was a lavish spender for those carefree penurious days. There were other Hebrew families who came and went during those days, but Wolf Rosenberg stayed on and founded a business which has the admiration, confidence, and respect of all the people to this day. When he first came to town, he started selling goods from door to door, out into the country and on up into Lake and Mendocino Counties. First he had a horse and light buggy for his merchandise and after a few successful trips, acquired a team and larger spring wagon, so after more profitable trips with this, he opened a store in town which year by year grew and prospered until it reached its present proportions. Mr. Rosenberg's success depended upon his honesty, friendliness, knowledge of people, and how to supply them with what they desired at a reasonable price. He was what might be called a born merchant, always dignified, always considerate, always square, yet always with an eye open for good business. That is why he prospered. Also he was never deaf to the call of the needy and did much for charity.

His sons, fine men all, like their father, have carried on the traditions and fine principles of their illustrious father, who was one of the outstanding figures in the upbuilding of the old hometown we all love so well.

LITTLE CHINA IN HEALDSBURG. My good friend Arthur Price, a native of Healdsburg, and for many years now on the editorial staff of the *San Francisco Examiner*, suggested a story about the Chinese in Healdsburg, who lived in the old hometown and did their share in keeping our clothes clean in the days of our youth, and to him thanks for the suggestion and for some of the information herein quoted.

Back in the days of main strength and awkwardness, before there were any steam laundries or automatic washing machines, the good housewives of Healdsburg, as in other places, did their washing via the old-fashioned washboard, tub, and hand wringer method, with plenty of hot water, soap-suds, and elbow grease. So it came to pass that Chinese laundries sprang up all over California, Healdsburg having two. Jo Wah Lee was the habitual proprietor of one located in an old wooden building between the city hall and Nosler's Skating Rink on Center Street and it did a thriving business. The other was operated by Sing Lee and was just behind Conner's Livery Stable, on posts or piling over the swampy ground on the east side of West Street near the slough. In earlier days John Marshall had a blacksmith shop on the site of the stable—he was the father of Anabelle and Marion Marshall, two of Healdsburg's most charming daughters. Many local business people patronized these two celestial laundries, their business was gigantic—in fact, they were an institution in the town; those who sent their washing to Jo Wah Lee thought they were getting the best service and proudly boasted of their superiority, while that portion whose clothes were cleansed by Sing Lee felt that they were getting more for their money and pity those who were not so blessed. There was a bit of rivalry between the two wash houses which reflected to the homes of their patrons.

There was always four to six "pig tails" (chinese) employed in each institution and both turned out perfectly beautiful laundry at a very nominal sum, and that was something in that day of many flounces, voluminous skirts, ruffled dresses, and drawers, to say nothing of stiff starched shirts, collars, and cuffs which were worn by the men. It was great fun to look in through their open door and watch them iron with their gigantic irons; first they would spread out the garment on the board, take a sip of water from a bowl, and spew this water in a fine spray all over the piece to moisten it and then proceed with the ironing, at the same time keeping up a string of conversation in Chinese. Their work, their customs, their language, in fact their whole ensemble, fascinated us small boys.

Arthur Price gives us a side light on the situation in a letter, part of which is quoted verbatim: "The town was rather well divided between those who took off Jo Wah Lee and those who followed the banners of Sing Lee. My grandmother, Mrs. Mulligan, was a patron of Jo Wah Lee, and we (the Andrew Price family) were devoted to Sing Lee. Each China New Year, the laundryman always brought huge bags of candies and nuts. These laundrymen were the town's Walter Winchells, and at times the Dun and

Bradstreets of the community." (Author's Note: For they saw all, heard all, knew all, and told what they thought best, also they knew who did and who did not pay their bills.)

My mother used to get rare from Sing Lee. She was very quick at Chinese dialect, and used to tell of Sing Lee's report on a current romance. From Jo Wah Lee's wash house a countryman named Ah Sing Lee, who conducted a fruit and vegetable business, carried his wares about town in two large baskets suspended by a bamboo pole which he balanced over his shoulder. His loads would weigh between three and four hundred pounds and he trotted from customer to customer with ease and grace, a happy smile spread over his countenance; a white man could not lift the load, for I have seen them try and fail, which greatly pleased Ah Sing. His business prospered for he was honest, friendly, and always appreciated a sale, no matter how small. He would usually have some small token for the children.

Besides the laundrymen and the vegetable peddler there was quite a number of their cousins employed as cooks at the two hotels and in private homes, and they always did the buying for their own departments, so the underground information bureau of the local Chinese had wide ramification.

At certain holidays they would fly beautiful kites with hummers, and shoot off long ropes of firecrackers, all of which gave the small boys of the town a great thrill. In addition to the candies and nuts, each patron was presented with a lily bulb which would grow and bloom in a bowl of water and pebbles; these were tokens of good luck to the house, the better the bloom the better the good luck.

The Chinese were our friends—we were kind to them—peace and confidence reigned between the Occident and the Orient. About 1875 Dennis Kearny, of San Francisco sand lot fame, started a campaign against the Chinese, who were beginning to do most of the labor in the state, sounding the slogan with clarion call, "Chinese Must Go," which finally culminated in the Chinese Exclusion Act by Congress, the measure being put through by our own congressman, Thomas J. Geary. Well, any movement, good or bad, if the proper amount of noise is made, gathers momentum, so a statewide effort to drive the "Chinks" from our shores got under way and was taken up by certain elements in our own town. Rocks were thrown at Chinamen on the streets, and sometimes when delivering clothes they would be assaulted and the clean clothes scattered in the dirt; of course the poor Chinaman would have to take them back and do them all over again or pay for those damaged beyond repair. At other times gangs of young men would collect a flock of ancient eggs, rotten vegetables, or some other obnoxious substance, and at night would gather in front of a laundry, have one of their number rap on the door, run out of range so that when the Chinaman opened the door the rest of the mob would give him a volley of garbage, much of which would get inside and foul up everything it came in contact with. The lives of the "Heathen" were made miserable, the old feeling of mutual trust and confidence faded, and even those Americans who continued to patronize them were hooted at. A steam laundry was started and the Chinese Wash House, along with the vegetable peddler, gradually became things of the past, and by 1900, the last of the old-time laundries closed its door forever.

Ed Passalacqua sold fresh vegetables from his wagon.

LA ITALIA. Turning back the pages of history, leaf by leaf, to those simple days of the late '70s and early '80s, we find the first influx of sturdy sons and daughters from sunny Italy. Among them were John Rosasco, Antonio Passalacqua, Frank Passalacqua, John Foppiano, Guiseppe Simi, Peter Gobbi, J.J. Gobbi, and Peter Alberigi. Most of the early Italian settlers came from northern Italy, were farmers, gardeners, and vineyardists, fine people, and all good citizens. Frank Passalacqua, the first, came to Cloverdale in the late '70s and purchased a few acres of land from Jake Heald, along the river bank near where McCray's station on the railroad is now located. He started a vegetable garden and of course prospered. Along about '79 or '80 Antonio Passalacqua, a brother of Frank, came to Healdsburg and purchased a part of the old Hudson ranch just south of town and Frank, having sold his Cloverdale property to a fellow countryman, came to Healdsburg and bought a part of the ranch from his brother, so they both went into the production of vegetables and strawberries. My father owned a ten-acre ranch cornering on the property of the Passalacquas, so we were, in a way, close neighbors and good friends.

John Foppiano acquired the old Dr. Cook ranch down the river road; for a long time lived in the the little house where I first saw the light of day in 1872. This house was later demolished as the Foppiano family prospered and a more imposing structure was erected to fit the needs of his growing family.

John Rosasco was one of the earliest farmers, vineyardists, and wine makers to come to our community and do his part in its upbuilding. Peter Alberigi and his family owned and operated an Italian hotel and boardinghouse on the west side of West Street. There was another similar institution in the old Terry property on the corner of Hayden and Fitch Streets, just across from the old North Methodist Church; on Sundays their boarders would make a lot of noise playing boccie ball. Peter Gobbi was another early settler from Italy and with his cousin, J.J. Gobbi, operated a large winery on the corner of West Street and Powell Avenue, in the '80s. Before that, this property was owned by an Englishman by the name of Ogalvy or Ogalvie. Giuseppe Simi, another pioneer Italian emigrant, owned large vineyards and operated one or two wineries and did much for the betterment of the town and spread the fame of its excellent wines.

Many Italians were drawn to our salubrious climate and fertile hills, and nearly all made good citizens as gardeners, farmers, vineyardists, hotel keepers, and later as business and professional men including doctors, lawyers, dentists, teachers, and engineers. The Italians prospered because they were not afraid of work and would be at it from dawn to dusk.

FIREMEN'S PICNICS. Back in the days when fair ladies wore bustles, hip pads, hair rats, false bangs, switches, and sometimes a pair of birds' nests to give them form and beauty, the Volunteer Firemen of Sonoma County used to hold an annual test of skill with their respective gadgets, which was always followed by a picnic and the absorption of more or less beer.

In each of the larger towns of the county there were hose companies and hook and ladder companies, all manned by patriotic public-spirited citizens, who gave their services for the good of the community as well as their personal glory. It also gave them a bit of prestige and standing among their fellow men. Then, too, all firemen were exempt from poll tax, which saved each $2 per year.

The firemen of Sonoma county and Healdsburg in particular were very loyal to and proud of their respective organizations. The hose company men wore red flannel shirts, white patent leather belts, and regulation firemen's helmets, decorated with the initials and number of their unit and the name of the town. The hook and ladder boys wore blue flannel shirts and caps, more in keeping with their particular job, and were they all, both hose and ladder men, all puffed up when they donned their uniforms and paraded with their hose cart or ladder wagon, both of which were pulled by hand. The hose company was composed mostly of Irishmen and Germans, among them being John McGuire, Pat Dempsey, Pat Lannan, Jim McClusky, the Schwab brothers, and many others who have been forgotten due to the lapse of half a century of time.

The hook and ladder boys, familiarly known as "The Hooks," were headed by a Mr. Logan, a Civil War veteran who had a shoe shop on the east side of the plaza. His two elder sons, Bob and Harry, Maitland Hall, Albert and Harry Garrett, Tab Young, and Will Dudley were some of the young men about town composing its members. They were proud of themselves and Healdsburg was proud of them for they frequently captured first prizes at the annual meets. They either kept the bacon at home or brought it back with them.

Once each year the firemen from various communities would meet in some town, have a parade in full regalia, with bands, banners, and broad-cloth, to strut their stuff and try to put it all over the other fellows. It happened that only once every four years was the celebration held in Healdsburg. After the parade, which was viewed by thousands of spectators from the sidewalks and other vantage points, each unit in turn

Will Dudley, shown here with his wife, Annie, was a volunteer fireman. Born in Napa in 1860, he moved to Healdsburg in 1874. He was later postmaster and a deputy sheriff before his death in 1924.

ran a hundred yards from a standing start, the hose men dragging their cart at utmost speed, the hydrant men pushing behind ready to pull the hose from the reel and couple it to the hydrant, and the pipe men ready to connect the nozzle when the length of hose was run out. By the time the nozzle was connected the spanner man at the hydrant would have the water turned on and flowing through the hose.

It took perfect timing to do all this in sequence and get a stream of water gushing from the nozzle without a miscue, for to win under such conditions a split second meant a lot. The hook and ladder boys would run a hundred yards as did the hose companies, pull an extension ladder from the truck, and start raising it the instant its foot touched the ground on the line, then extend the ladder, which was no small feat.

If the ladder man was too quick, the ladder would be over-balanced and down it would come; if too slow, some other ladder company would be the winner. So the timing of all these details had to be exactly right to the hundredth part of a second or to a gnat's whisker. Bob Logan, being light and active, was Healdsburg's ladder man and could climb the ladder like a streak of greased light. Maitland Hall and Harry Garrett were the lead men on the end of the rope, as they were the swiftest runners, and could set a furious pace.

The expertness with which both branches of the fire department could execute these acts was the eighth wonder of the world. Winning teams were given appropriate trophies amid the plaudits of the populace. Then all would repair to the picnic grounds where solid, semi-solid, and liquid refreshments were lavishly dispensed and copiously consumed amid music and laughter, all having a grand and glorious good time.

The rivalry was keen, the good fellowship generous, but sometimes slight altercations would result in fist fights, with little damage to the participants because more sober minds would step in and quell the combatants, and the day would end in glory. Those were the great days in which the people made the most of their opportunities and took a pride in their work and play, enjoying themselves and holidays.

HORSEMEN. The Paxtons, the Warfields, the Wattles, the Lathrops, the Gums, the Zanes, the Van Allens, and many other families prided themselves on the fine horses and nobby rigs they turned out. Those sleek, high-headed, high-stepping, speedy horses with silver or polished brass mountings and plenty of white rings on the harness were truly a picture when combined with snappy carts, buggies, surries, traps or coaches; no wonder they were all puffed up.

Even my father, whose ways were simple, had a mare and surry with silk fringe all around the canopy top. It was quite a nice outfit and Fanny, the mare, could travel quite comfortably herself.

Wolf Rosenberg and T.S. Merchant each owned and drove a high-spirited speedy horse to lightside bar Brewster buggies—they each took a bit of justified pride in their respective turnouts.

In those backwoods days of our simple innocence the roads were dirt and a bit longer than our present paved highways; they were horse-and-buggy roads; now we have auto roads and even what few horses we have ride in trailers.

A bunch of the local boys who loved to gamble on anything and horses in particular, offered to bet Mr. Rosenberg $250 that he could not drive his horse to Santa Rosa in one hour and fifteen minutes. The wager was promptly taken, necessary preliminaries were looked after, and at the appointed hour, Mr. Rosenberg started on his record drive.

The time of departure was telegraphed to the judges in Santa Rosa so no errors could creep in. The drive was completed in just one hour and fourteen minutes, according to the timekeeper's watch. So Mr. Rosenberg took the $250 the boys had bet him, slowly drove his fine dark bay mare home, and lived happily ever after.

Now this exploit of Mr. Rosenberg roused T.S. Merchant to action, for he felt sure that his horse Gladdy was the best horse in Sonoma County on and off the track and he itched to show him off so he naturally began to boast a bit about his horse. This was done to tempt a bet by some of the local sports and it worked.

Again a bet of $250 was made but this time the time limit was cut to one hour flat. The betting crowd thought they had Mr. Merchant up a tree and out on a limb, they just chuckled with glee at the thought of recouping their previous losses.

Instead of using a buggy, Mr. Merchant hitched his pet horse to a very light, high-wheeled road cart almost as flimsy as a track sulky. As before, all necessary details for the race against time were looked after. The start was made, the time of departure was telegraphed to Santa Rosa, and the contest was on.

Mr. Merchant reached his goal, drove once around the old courthouse, and came to a stop in front of the judges. The horse gave a few deep breaths, then breathed easily and appeared ready to start back; he was not even jaded. Time? Oh yes, the time was fifty-nine minutes. Once more the past glory of Healdsburg's ancient history is recalled.

Note—to F. M. Cooper of Santa Rosa, a good horseman, who has spent seventy-eight of his more than eighty years on earth in Sonoma County, the author is indebted for some of the facts in this story.

And the horse Gladdy? Well, one month later Mr. Cooper purchased him from Mr. Merchant and owned him for twenty years. The last few years of this noble horse's life were spent in a pleasant pasture reflecting, no doubt, on his past glory until he became so old and decrepit Mr. Cooper had him killed to put him out of his misery.

THE KINGDOM OF HEALDSBURG. The kingdom of Healdsburg was not like the kingdom of Heaven, from everlasting to everlasting—it was transitory, for a day only, but what a day. This temporary monarchy was way back in the '80s; perhaps it was on May 1, 1886, in the days when men were brave and ladies very modest.

J.M. Alexander and C.B. Pond were editors and publishers of the *Healdsburg Enterprise* at that time; R.K. Truitt owned and operated the local theatre; A.W. Garrett and Ed Haigh, all these and many other prominent citizens, most of whom are long since gone to their home on high were on the committee or took part in the pageant.

Felix Mulgrew, a local realtor and assemblyman, was chosen king, as Rex Felix I, and that exquisite young lady, Ann O'Connor, a particularly charming and beautiful brunette, was his queen for the day. King Felix and Queen Ann had knights, ladies, chamberlains, courtiers, heralds, ladies in waiting, pages, jesters, and men at arms,

Alice Haigh (Dixon), center, ruled as queen of the Healdsburg Floral Festival in May of 1896. Seated to her left is Zoe Bates (Fuller); seated to her right is Nettie Barnes (Chisholm). Standing, from left to right, are Violet Luedke (Smith), Edna Biddle (Stone), Nellie Petray (Lawrence), and Lena Zane (Purvine). The attending pages are Bert McDonough (left) and Van Whitney (right), and the princess is little Julia Mehrtens.

in fact the personnel of a royal court. They were dressed in gorgeous costumes of the time of King Arthur of the Round Table and made a dazzling and colorful spectacle. The king and queen were seated on a royal float drawn by four white horses and decorated with flowers, greenery, and bunting; each wore a golden crown made of gilt paper and pasteboard, emblazoned with colored glass for jewels, and carried scepters of more or less the same materials. The illusion was perfect.

They made an inspiring sight when surrounded by their court, mounted on gaily caparisoned fiery chargers, knights with lances and banners, preceded by four mounted heralds with trumpets. Old King Cole had nothing on them when it came to splendor.

The cavalcade formed downtown and, headed by the incomparable Sotoyome Band, marched majestically between lines of cheering subjects out Matheson Street to Seaman's Pasture, where the tournament was to be held.

"The Field of the Cloth of Gold" was not in it compared to the kingdom of Healdsburg when it came to a gorgeous display of youth and beauty, brave men and fair ladies, pomp and ceremony. The royal cortege drew up opposite a grandstand that had been erected for the spectators, the band played, the knights paraded and a fanfare of trumpets called for attention, when King Felix I, supported by his gracious, smiling queen, read the royal proclamation declaring this a holiday to be given over to pleasure and feasting. All sorrow and dull care was banished from the realm; joy and gladness were to reign supreme.

A series of decorated arches had been erected from which a pendant supported an iron ring which could be easily picked off with a lance. The knights who were to ride for glory this day would poise their lances according to ancient custom and at the sound of the bugle would charge full tilt, ride under the arches, and endeavor to catch the rings with their lances as they passed by.

It was a great tournament, a wonderful display of skill, daring, and horsemanship. The knight who succeeded in getting the most rings with his lance was the winner and hero of the day and received an appropriate gift from the hands of the lovely queen. Prizes were awarded to the other contestants in order of their skill for there were twenty riders in the lists that memorable day.

Their names—well, many of them have been forgotten but the following still remain on memory's page: R.K. Truitt, George Haigh, Ed Haigh, James Seawell, Guy Wolcott, Summers Brumfield, Bailhache, Strong, Grant, and many others.

Of course there were peanuts, popcorn balls, pink lemonade, candy, and other devices for refreshment befitting such an outstanding celebration.

It was a great day that has gone down in history as an event that had never before been equaled and only once since, when on May 1, 1896, another similar event took place place when Miss Alice Haigh was queen and her brother Jack distinguished himself as one of Healdsburg's four great stars. The charming and beautiful Queen Ann taught in the public school in the late '80s and early '90s, then became Mrs. Wood Wattles. She was admired and loved by all who knew her. (The writer is indebted to Arthur Price for the information in this tale.)

FEED MY LAMBS. It was back in Sunday school days when hours seemed days in length and Thanksgiving, Christmas, New Years Day, May Day, and the Fourth of July seemed years apart and would never come again.

Those great days of celebration were outstanding events in our young lives and with what longing and eager participation we looked forward to the arrival of each succeeding event, for it meant thrills, excitement, and unbounded joy.

In those days May Day was always fittingly celebrated by the townspeople enmasse, by the public school, or by one or all of the local Sunday schools with a picnic. These picnics might be held on top of Fitch Mountain, under the shade of Adam and Eve, in Seaman's Pasture, Hassett's Grove, or out Mill Creek way by the old gristmill, and what simple, innocent fun we all did have, our happiness knew no bounds.

Our parents, our teachers, and our pastors all went along to provide the lunches, homemade ice cream, and, if necessary, when the way was long, transportation, as well as to keep us out of mischief.

Our teachers and preachers to ride herd on us lest we stray from the straight and narrow path or accidentally break one of the Ten Commandments. Anyway, we had a day of pleasure out in the open air or under the shade of the beautiful trees and it did us good.

When lunch was finally served, which seemed to take hours, one of the divines present would ask a blessing and the whole gathering might join in singing that grand old hymn, which starts off with "Praise God from whom all Blessings Flow," then with joy in our hearts and an aching void in our tummies we would light into the sumptuous repast and eat and eat until we could hold no more and what a capacity and appetites healthy youngsters can develop.

In looking back over those golden days one particular event stands out on memories page—it happened on a May Day in the early '80s and was a union Sunday school picnic, held out in the grove section of Seaman's Pasture, in which all Sunday schools of the protestant churches joined.

The meeting place was in front of the old Plaza Church and at the appointed hour all the respective Sunday schools assembled with their teachers, preachers, families, banners, and enthusiasm. Of course the older preachers, teachers, and our parents rode out to the picnic grounds in horse-drawn vehicles on many varieties and states of preservation, from farm wagons to fine carriages. Even the horses were not forgotten, for under the seats with the lunches or tied on behind were sacks of hay and bags of grain for the animals, for this was still in the so-called ox cart or horse-and-buggy days, when people were civilized.

The Sunday school from the old North Methodist Church was out in full force and Mrs. Susan B. Currier's class of very good boys was accorded the honor of carrying the banner as they had the best average attendance for the past year. This banner was quite ornate, a white field about two by three feet, trimmed with blue silk and fringes; in its center was a picture or representation of a wooly lamb, its legs tucked under it and resting peacefully.

Above the recumbent lamb in capital letters was MESS, which stood for Methodist Episcopal Sunday School, and below the emblem of innocence were the words "Feed my Lambs," a very appropriate motto for such an auspicious occasion, for at the picnic that day we were to be fed to the point of super saturation, both spiritually and bodily.

This banner was supported by a cross tree hanging from a staff made from old curtain poles with the polished brass balls on the tips to add to its beauty, along with the fringe, cords, and tassels, and from the top of the pole, four long streamers or ribbons were fastened to be used as guys when it was being carried.

Why, no one ever knew, but it fell to my lot to carry the banner, while each of the four streamers were held by Bert Soules, Dellie Hassett, George Curtiss, and Will Pride, some color guard, and were we five boys proud-pouter pigeons, strutting goblers and vain peacocks could not have been more swelled up or elated.

While waiting for the line of march to form, some of the older boys who did not attend Sunday school gathered to watch and sneer at the good little Sunday school boys. Among other things they wanted to know what kind of mess we were going to feed our lambs and other taunting remarks which, of course, roused our anger and made us feel like fighting but we were told by our dear pastor to pay no attention to them as they were bad boys, no doubt being tempted by the devil.

The march out Matheson Street to the pasture was colorful and decorous, we did not even sing "Onward Christian Soldiers," which would have been appropriate.

The day was a great success for after the morning exercises which included a Maypole dance, recitations, tableaus, singing songs of May, and a picnic lunch of gigantic size with all the choicest viands of the season, including whole flocks of cold fried chicken, and having eaten until we could hold no more we rested in the shade for a spell with the rest of the afternoon devoted to harmless games such as drop the handkerchief, tag, some races, but no kissing games; such things were reserved for the more worldly picnics.

About four in the afternoon the picnic party would break up, the good people returning to their homes since they all had work to do. They would be tired, happy, and with all the lambs well fed.

THE OWL CLUB. Just had a call from an old-time Healdsburger, Mrs. C.R. Forge, who was Onie Mulligan back in those good old days, and with her was her charming daughter who lives with her in their Santa Clara home.

This delightful lady had with her two old scrap books with items of interest harking back to those days of the late '60s and on down through the years. It was thrilling to rummage through the yellow pages and muse on persons and events that took place when a small boy in the old hometown.

Among the outstanding features socially in the early '80s were such things as the Albanian Club, devoted to literature and dramatics and from the records in the old scrap book the young people of that day sure knew how to have fun and entertain themselves.

Cantatas, dramas, minstrels, grand balls, masquerades, and other forms of entertainment by local talent and all the young people in general were regular events, along with parties in private homes, picnics, and hay rides.

The Owl Club, organized in the year 1883, was perhaps the most spectacular of those days and perchance there may be a few of the old-timers around who will recall with pleasure the splendor of the parties, arranged by this flock of night birds.

They would have mask balls, fancy dress balls, hard time balls, and on one occasion a kindergarten ball where all the participants both masculine and feminine were dressed as little boys and girls. Some had schoolbooks, dolls, marbles, and other childish toys to add reality to the scene and what a rollicking good time they had.

Some of the boys had patches sewed on the seats of their pants and knees or their elbows to be realistic for at that time in our history many small boys wore patched clothes to school.

One young sport, whose name is forgotten, asked a lady friend to place patches on knees and seat of a pair of perfectly good pants and she, taking him literally, cut out squares and dexterously sewed in the desired patches, making a perfectly beautiful job all to the ruination of the Sunday breeches.

As a small boy viewing the ensemble from the gallery I still recall how funny

C.B. Pond looked dressed in knee pants and short coat with school satchel, primer, and slate. Another young man was barefoot with a big toe bandaged with a dirty rag to simulate a small boy with a sore toe.

In those golden days an event of that kind was an all-night affair, with a midnight banquet at one of the hotels and the price per couple was usually $5. There was a world of difference between the pageantry of that time and tawdry 50¢ dances of the present modern period; the boys of those days were real sports, nothing was too good for their ladies, and how they did spread themselves.

With many other small boys it was a pleasure to watch some of these displays of flaming youth and lovely ladies from the gallery of Truitt's Theatre and later when in my teens to participate in some of the festal events.

The membership roll of the Owl Club included nearly all the young bloods and charming ladies of the period so a complete list of them would fill a lot of space. Among the moving spirits were Julius Alexander and his cousin Carrie, Arthur Mulligan and his sister Onie, Harvey Peck, Jonas Bloom, John Wilson, C.B. Pond, the Willey sisters, Emma Thompson, and others.

Also noted are such names as Barth, Joy, Thing, Brotherton, McManus, Gaines, Cook, Young, Garrett, Seawell, Rickman, Truitt, Sears, O'Connor, Riley, West, Grant, Bailhache, Emerson, Traynor, Nichols, and Brown; what a galaxy and what good times they had.

Speaking of Mrs. Forge, who was Onie Mulligan, she was one of the outstanding ladies of the time, full of fun, with all the wit and charm of her Hibernian ancestors and a favorite with all. As a small boy, she appeared to me to be a wonderful lady and in meeting her the other day after an interval of over fifty years she is as charming, as snappy, her mind as clear, her sense of humor as keen, and her memory as accurate now in her eighties as when she was one of the belles of the ball in the days of our callow youth.

Time marches on in this changing world but we can all get a bit of pleasure by recalled persons, places, and events of a bygone era.

(This was written by Dr. Shipley in 1941.)

IOGT. Back in the days of slow motion, those horse-and-buggy days or even to the days of the creaking wooden wheeled ox cart, there was a tendency on the part of the population to be up to date and a little ahead.

Take our modern alphabetic soup, stew and hash such as WPA, FHLB, AAA, CMP, FHA, FYA, TVA, RSVP, QED, with a million more and we might add OMD, which stands for Old Maids Day, for they should have a day all their own. The old-timers were on to their job as to the use of letters we learned as A B C's.

We had and revered such combinations of letters as GAR, WCTU, WRC, AOUW, AOMC, IOOF, B of H (Band of Hope) F and AM, CE, last but not least the IOGT, that ancient and honorable institution known as the Independent Order of Good Templars, a very rabid temperance society, now like the dinosaurs extinct, but in those hectic days and age a force to be reckoned with. Even though the lady members were denied their sacred right and privilege of going to the polls and casting their ballots against Demon Rum.

Carrie Alexander, the daughter of Cyrus Alexander, was a moving spirit in the Owl Club. (From a chalk portrait owned by Lucille Alexander Clark.)

Great parties and campaigns these good people would sponsor. They met in a rather dingy old hall or lodge room above the store of J.B. Prince, then located directly across the street from the city hall. Old Dad Proctor, father of Chas. and Bill Proctor, was its most shining light and vehement exponent.

Mrs. Susan B. Currier, my Sunday school teacher, was also among its most ardent supporters. She was also an enthusiastic WCTU, and CE, as were many other good citizens and citizenettes who abhorred his Satanic Majesty, Old King Alcohol. So you see, the New Deal with its multiplicity of meaningless conglomerations of letters from Alpha to Omega had nothing on the deformers, reformers, and performers of those dear old days that are gone, for history repeats itself over and over again from everlasting to ever-lasting.

If Adam had had a following of nuts, cranks, sobsisters, joykillers, wisecrackers, jayhockers, psalmsingers, and etc. to follow his lead, no doubt he would have had hieroglyphics smeared all over the Garden of Eden and thus end of another lesson.

THE SINGING SCHOOLS. In our infancy, when our parents were young people in their 20s and 30s with all the world before them, as it has been for many of us and now is for our sons and daughters and soon will be for our grandchildren, who are fast growing up, pastime and pleasure has and will be an important element in the lives of most people.

Some get their elation attending divine services or protracted meetings, others enjoy getting a "snootful" of ardent spirits, still others sit in the sun or shade smoking their pipes and resting themselves, some enjoy one form of diversion and some another, but the majority got satisfaction doing a good job well and were not afraid of work from daylight to dark when they would be ready for play.

All these forms of work and refreshment would be too vast to catalog, but the old fashioned singing school (singin' schule as it was often called by old-timers) helped break the monotony of the long winter evenings and did those who attended a power of good, for music is a safety valve for pent up emotions. There were choral societies and other forms of musical diversion, but it took the traveling singing teachers to "cop" the prizes and carry away the "dough."

These outfits usually were composed of a man and wife, both of pleasing personality, well versed in music and possessed of the gift of "gab," especially the man, who conducted the instructions. The lady member of the team usually was the accompanist, demure and very charming. They usually had a song book to sell, and singing lessons, including the song book, cost $2 to $2.50 per person, two or more from the same family at greatly reduced rates. Their classes were well attended and the clean-up profitable.

It was along about the same time that a fuzzy down began to appear on some of our boyish faces that a Professor Randell and his wife, Lollie, blew into town with a burning desire to sell song books and teach singing as it should be taught. In no time they rounded up a big class, for Randell was tall, dark, and handsome with fine manners and a marvelous voice. Lollie was exquisite, dainty as a flower, pretty as a picture, and could pound the ivories to a fare-you-well. They were a good team.

There's no business like show business—performers from an early show strike a pose. (Courtesy Vivian Hall, Healdsburg Museum collection.)

Their class was held in the North Methodist Church, for which they paid a nominal rental. The Wednesday night prayer meeting for that week was held in the parsonage to accommodate the charming Randells. There must have been close to one hundred singers in the school, divided into four sections: tenors, sopranos, altos, and bassos. The bassos far outnumbered tenors, for many did not sing much better than crows, but they bought a book and joined the school for the fun as all were welcome who had the price.

About the same time instruction was to start, Lollie would be very busy talking to some of the lady singers, the professor would rap for order and instruct the class to say in unison, "Class say, Come Lollie," which they would do with a will, and of course, Lollie would come, take her place at the organ, and the storm or sound of music was on in full force.

After the second evening the class beat the professor to it and as soon as he rapped for order the whole crowd would shout as one, "Class say, Come Lollie," which caused a bit of fun, made Lollie blush, and the professor smile. And so they came, they saw, they conquered and departed, leaving the community happier and more expert in psalmody. Way back in the early '70s, according to my mother, a Professor Baxter was not only a good singer, but he was a marvelous whistler, his wife would play and he would whistle, outwhistling the birds. He was to teach singing and whistling all for the price of the song book and the five lessons. On the opening night after giving a demonstration of his whistling, he announced that he would start instructions; solemnly rapping for order he said, "Now class, I am about to instruct you in the art of whistling, attention please," and without cracking a smile, he said, "Class, prepare to pucker," at which time he would pucker his lips and the class, instead of following his instructions, would go into gales of laughter.

He would call for order and try it over with the same result, so after three or four attempts to get his class to pucker, he would say, "Well, we had better get on with our singing lesson as the class is unable to pucker and if you cannot pucker you cannot whistle." From then on until ten o'clock the singing instructor went on without interruption or puckering.

Each evening the same act took place, with the same results, until the last evening when one man asked how it was they received no whistling lessons, to which Prof. Baxter replied he was willing but how could he teach people to whistle who laughed instead of puckering, and so the incident was passed off.

Thus the rounds of events followed one and another in the early days of the old hometown as time marched on. The simple pleasures and diversions of that day would now be looked upon with disdain.

AN ORANGE RACE. Around 1884, a Mr. Nosler moved into town and erected a roller skating rink almost across the street from Truitt's Theatre, where skating on the little wooden wheels had been in progress some time, each afternoon and evening, Sundays excepted or when some show came to town or a local organization gave a ball or held a festival. Skating was quite the rage with young and old alike, and many people spent much of their spare time at the rink on rollers, having the time of their lives, wheeling, circling, dipping, gliding, and falling down.

The new opposition rink created a bit of heated rivalry and each proprietor tried to outdo the other with novel entertainment to attract the crowd. They would have costume parties, calico and rag parties, pie races, egg and spoon races, three-legged races, and, on rare occasions, have a fancy skater demonstrate grace and agility, all on the little spinning wheels.

On one occasion Brother Nosler advertised an orange race by two novices who had never been on skates before, participants to be selected from the audience. It drew a big crowd, for the idea was novel and never had been tried before, it was something new.

When the time came in the evening for the race to be pulled off, the floor was cleared of skaters, two boxes of big, juicy oranges were placed at the head of the hall about twenty feet apart, assistants began placing the oranges in two rows at about three-foot intervals, until the long parallel lines of oranges extended from each box to the front of the hall. Excitement ran high for some real fun was in store.

Mr. Nosler called for two volunteers from among the boys who had never been on skates before, to come forward. A prize of $1 would be given the winner of the race, which was great riches in those poverty-stricken days. As none of the boys seemed anxious to risk their necks, Mr. Nosler went among a bunch of small boys standing near the door and collared Lester Gale and this narrator. Nosler saw we were green and had never been on skates in our lives. He proudly marched us up between the orange boxes, gave each a pair of skates, and announced that we were to start by skating to the far end, bring back the oranges one at a time, place them in the box and so continue until the last orange had been gathered, also that we had to skate and not run or walk.

We removed our coats, buckled on the skates, were placed in readiness and were told to start at the blast of a whistle. Then he said, "are you ready," gave an ear-splitting blast of an old police whistle and the race was on, or off, as the case might be. Each contestant succeeded in reaching the end of the line of oranges without a mishap and then fell "kerplop" like a thousand bricks to the floor, picking up an orange, struggled to his feet, and started back to the box.

It was a great race and the audience went wild with joy as one or the other or both the contestants took a nasty spill or sat down "kersog" upon an orange—and how the juice did squirt—the squashed fruit had to be picked up and returned to the box along with the whole oranges, nothing must be left behind but the juice which could not be recovered.

The seats of our trousers sopped with orange juice, our clothes dirtied, perspiration exuding as with wild gesticulations and repeated falls, we continued to refill the boxes. Sometimes in falling an orange would be rolled to one side of the hall and would have to be recovered, which added to the work of the races and the hilarity of the spectators. And how they did laugh, clap their hands, and cheer as some outlandish mishap befell either of us.

We all had a lot of fun along with the bumps and bruises. Lester won the race by one macerated orange and received the prize (a silver dollar) amid the plaudits and laughter of the fans. Mr. Nosler gave the loser a 50¢ piece as a consolation, which was very magnanimous on his part and showed his heart was in the right place; perhaps he felt sorry for the bruises received.

On reaching home, proud as a peacock over the four bits, all dirty and soaked with orange juice as well as bruised from head to foot, my parents gave me a good dressing down for being such a sap and ruining a pair of perfectly good pants, as it was, perhaps luck was with me that no teeth were lost or bones broken.

"PLAY BALL." The umpire's clarion call, "Play Ball," thrilled us in the days of our youth as it does even to the present day, for when it comes to playing ball the moderns have nothing on the old-timers. Way back some fifty or sixty years ago, we old-time Healdsburgers were as enthusiastic over the great national game as are the more blase moderns; only we were a bit archaic.

The small boys in the primary grades of school played numbers, one- and two-old cat, in and out, and anti over, with homemade bats and balls or an occasional solid rubber ball which would bounce and bounce and bounce. The girls played the same games with soft balls and flat bats and they had a heap of fun, if noise was any gauge to go by, for they did a lot of treble screeching. We boys used to play in the school yard recesses and at noon, and, before the days of the canneries, out in Seaman's Pasture, and in dead-end streets; Saturday and Sunday afternoons and behind the old North Methodist Church in the hitching lot after school and on Saturday when baseball season was on.

The big boys and young men of the town, Al and Harry Garrett, Tom and Teb Young, the Cook boys, the Grant boys, the Bailhache boys, Lou Norton, and later on

Quim Sewell, Harry Meyer, George Remmel of Geyserville, Rainey Haigh, Charles Bond, Lieu Hall, and Jack Taueffer were among some of the outstanding players of the so-called big league games played with contending teams from out of town.

After the high school was established, with H.R. Bull as headmaster, there sprang up a bit of rivalry between the younger boys of the Advent College and the high school, so once each year a championship game was played in Seaman's Pasture. These games were well attended by enthusiastic rooters for both sides, verbal mud would be thrown back and forth, and on rare occasions the temperature rose so high that a fist fight ensued.

In the early days of the high school, Bert Haigh and Julius Fried were in the upper or first class and Lydon Shaw, Tom Sullivan, Melville Rosenberg, John Barnes, Marvin Vaughan, Charles Bond, Grant Cook, Rainey Haigh, and this narrator were in the second or freshman class, so to make up a team with substitutes we had to take a few of the larger boys of the grammar school. Later on as the school grew in strength these games became quite a feature of the scholastic year.

The big league boys of the town used to play the big league boys from the Advent College and these games were picturesque with plenty of verbal banter hurled back and forth, though the Advent boys did not indulge in cuss words. Arthur Price tells of an interesting game he witnessed in which the coach for the Advent boys was trying to rattle the town boys pitcher by repeating in as sneering a manner as he knew how, "he's got a paper arm, he's got butter fingers, and he don't love Jesus."

Sometime in the mid-'80s during the height of the ball season in the grammar school, girls were playing a very hotly contested game and as a result of a disputed point two of the girls, Sylvia Hart and Lena Hughes, got into a rough and tumble that was a honey. The girls were both big, strong, and well balanced and full of fight any old time and how they did make the hair, cuticle, and clothes fly for a few minutes with all the school kids yelling and urging their favorite on with all they possessed. It came near being a general free for all, but was stopped by Prof. Ennis and several of the lady teachers, who were, or seemed to be, horrified by such unseemly conduct but no doubt within their innermost souls they were thrilled. All the kids were, for they put up a lusty series of cheers, howls, and cat calls.

A bit of praise for those old-time ball players who helped to add spice to our humdrum existence in those peaceful, ignorant days. It gives me pleasure to express my thanks to many old friends who have written giving me tips on almost forgotten persons and events of school days in the old hometown, would we all get together again for a talkfest and a hand shake as well as a kind word for those who have journeyed into the everlasting.

THE BAND OF HOPE. Back in the good old days, in the '80s, in addition to the IOGT and the WCTU, both hide-bound, rock-ribbed temperance societies for the grown-ups, we had the Band of Hope for the young people. This organization died a natural death in about 1886 or 1887.

The Albanian Literary and Military Society was a major social club in Healdsburg. Shown here in 1885, from left to right, are as follows: (front row) Minnie Reynolds McMullin, Emma Truitt Petry, May Shaw, and Artie Griest; (back row) Emma Logan Beeson, Millie Emerson Phillips, Sara Sullivan Ross, and an unidentified drummer.

This society would meet Sunday afternoon at about three o'clock, holding their sessions in the different Protestant churches; it was something along the line of a Sunday school. We had a Gigadier Brindel or a straw-boss who opened the ceremonies with due solemnity and the chaplain would offer a prayer. I can remember well how reverently John Barnes would read the prayer from the ritual book. We used to sing several temperance songs set to the music of some of those grand old hymns found in the Gospel Hymn book, one of which, part of the closing ceremony, ran as follows: "yield not to temptation for weakness is sin, each victory will help you some other to win, fight manfully onward, dark passions subdue; look ever to Jesus, he will carry you through; etc." We would have lessons on the evil of intemperance and the dire effects of alcohol on the human body, mind, and soul.

Each Sunday all present would renew their oath of allegiance to the cause of temperance which would end up with "God helping me, I faithfully promise to forever abstain from the use of intoxicating liquors as a beverage, including wine, beer and cider so help me God. Amen." Sad to say a few of the enthusiastic Band of Hope Boys did forget their oath of sobriety and became slaves to old King Alcohol.

Another thing that was stressed was the use of tobacco, especially the smoking of cigarettes as in those days it was only human degenerates and under-world characters who indulged in their use. I can remember how Mrs. W.G. Swan, who at that time

69

practiced law in Healdsburg, and occasionally imbibed more of the cup that queers than was good for her, used to rant and rave about the evils of intemperance and the degeneracy produced by use of cigarettes. She would describe a cigarette as "the filthy weed rolled up in a foul paper with fire at one end and a fool at the other."

Some of the rabid-antis of that day made the statement that both tobacco and cigarette papers were loaded with opium so as to get a firmer hold on tobacco users. There might have been a glimmer of truth in this statement, for that was long before the Pure Food Law and National Narcotic Act.

Others of the older people who used to be regular attendants at these gatherings and lent their forceful moral support in the fight against the Demon Rum and the Lady Nicotine were the ministers of several churches. In some cases their good wives would join them. Uncle Charles and Aunty Achsah Alexander and Mrs. Susan Currier were among those always present as was old Dad Proctor, who was the big tycoon of temperance societies.

To some of us good little Sunday school boys, these meetings, while a diversion and a chance to meet and admire the girls, were sometimes a nuisance, for if the weather was fine and we wanted to go swimming or hunt birds' eggs or hunt birds with sling shots on a Sunday afternoon we got into trouble, for we had to attend these meetings— our parents saw to that.

Every dog has his day, so the old story goes, and we who remember these old events had ours. And now as we walk down the glorious pathway of life to the setting sun and journey's end, we can look back with pleasant recollections upon many of these happenings, that at the time seemed an awful bore or an unnecessary oppression of our liberty to romp and frisk, and play as our desires dictated.

Perhaps if modern parents and neighbors gave as much of their time to the rearing of the youth of the land as did our forbears, we might have less juvenile delinquency. So with a bit of a tribute to those grand persons who earnestly endeavored to mold our characters in the way they should go, thus endeth another lesson in ancient history.

ANY MORE WOULD GO FLIPITY FLOPITY. It was back in those grassy green days in the fall of 1879 that the following play on words took place. I know the story is true for my mother used to tell it as a good joke on a female cousin of hers and I know mother would not deviate from the truth.

As told before it was in the spring of 1870 that my mother, then a young lady of twenty summers, came to Healdsburg with her mother and sister Isabelle and shortly after, mother's maternal grandparents, Mr. and Mrs. James Wood, with several of their sons and daughters who came from Cornellville, New York state, having been lured by the glowing accounts of climate, soil, and golden opportunities to be had in the then-primitive village.

A few years before, Stephen Wood, an elder son of James Wood, with his family, had moved to Oregon and taken up land in that wilderness and was prospering. They had in those days as did other families a flock of offspring and among them a charming daughter, Nina, about the age of my mother and as they had been chums back in the states, of course Nina had to make the trip to Healdsburg with her family to see her grandparents, uncles, aunts, and cousins.

In those pre-modern days folks used to visit around a lot; it was the custom and everybody had a good time, visitees and visitors alike. Also in those early days most folks were polite and proper and did things just according to the rules of social custom. My mother's people gave a party for cousin Nina and she made quite a hit with all the younger set, she had a simple charm and was pleasant to look upon. Of course she was invited to parties to be given in her honor by some of mother's friends.

Having lived for some time in the backwoods of Oregon, cousin Nina appealed to my grandmother who was very strict, decorous, and proper for a bit of coaching in good manners.

Always at those parties in early days a sumptuous dinner was served with everything but the pie placed on the table in copious quantities and one could eat his or her fill, capacity was the limit.

These dinners were an essential part of entertainment, food was cheap, cooks were good, wood was plentiful, so the cost of a table groaning under the weight of viands was minimal.

Now Nina wanted to know just how to act and what to say so as not to display the fact that she was a green country girl; among other things Grandmother Dutcher informed her that if she was asked to have her plate refilled (generous helpings to start with being the usual thing) she should say "No I thank you, I have eaten sufficiently, any more would be superfluity."

So sweet Nina with the other girls and boys went to the party given by a neighbor family in her honor and of course after partaking freely of the good things of the table and being the guest of honor her gracious host asked her to have a second helping. Nina blushed, hesitated, looked baffled as though she was trying to recall something of vital importance, and she was panicky for she was desperately trying to recall her aunt's instruction on propriety.

A great light illumined her lovely face, a sparkle came into her violet eyes, a sweet smile parted her ruby lips, and she said, "No thank you sir, I have eaten insufficiently, any more would go flipity flopity." Of course everybody laughed thinking it was a witticism on her part, but poor Nina almost collapsed, yet being a good sport rallied to the situation and joined in the round of merriment even if she did almost cry her heart out after going home to spend the night with my mother. (An illustration of what dire calamities may follow a simple lapse in language.)

THE TORCH BEARERS. Ever since man emerged from primeval chaos and descended from the jungles and took to the open spaces as lord and master of things terres-trial, the light of a torch has been one of the prized possessions and gave him a thrill. For countless ages his only means of artificial illumination was a pine knot, a brand from the limb of a tree, or a bundle of reeds soaked in pitch, when lighted by the tedious process of making fire by rubbing two dry sticks of wood together.

After whale oil and later coal came into use, more modern devices for such purposes were being used and along the time of the Civil War and later, men took to parading the streets at night in honor of some person, event, or to stir up political enthusiasm, each man carrying a lighted torch and strutting proud as a peacock. These spectacles were impressive and gave the admiring populace all great pleasure. They were quite a sight, especially when hundreds of men and sometimes thousands of them marched four abreast, in sections and divisions, with flags flying, banners floating, transparencies, floats, some with Greek Fire (red fire), each man with a torch and a pocketful of roman candles to add a shower of sparks and shooting stars to the magnificence of the pageant.

There was one of these torches in the attic of our home on Hayden Street, which my father carried in many local torch light processions in Healdsburg. It was one of my cherished possessions. During political campaigns it was the custom back in the '70s, '80s and '90s to have rallies in every town in the county, for which the railroad would run special trains, bringing thousands of enthusiastic supporters. When it was held in Healdsburg special trains would run from Petaluma, Santa Rosa, Cloverdale, and all way stations so the people could whoop-it-up, see the sights, and make a great noise.

Also after an election the local fans of the winning side would hold a ratification or jubilation, with a torch light parade, bonfires at the streetcorners, the local bands, the firing of anvils, and at one time the old brass gun, shouts of victory and yells or derision for the vanquished, and all the other trappings with speeches by spell-binding orators, singing, etc., in Truitt's Theatre to wind up the celebration.

In the story, "A Near Accident," published in the *Tribune* May 2, 1940, was told how a small boy placed a rock in the old brass gun which was being fired in honor of Benjamin Harrison's election to the presidency and how the rock described a howling parabola across the plaza and crashed through the front window of the Ruffner Store just over the heads of the crowd, which was just one incident in the history of the old hometown.

All these events took place in the days before modern thought, trends, and sophistication, government regulation, alphabetic restrictions, and cockeyed questionnaires and screwball reports, when men were free and time hung heavy on their hands when work was done. How times, conditions, desires, and recreations have changed from the simple, honest pleasures of our boyhood to this up-to-date and way ahead modern time. One wonders sometimes are we progressing or retrogressing? Thus endeth another lesson in ancient history with an unanswerable question.

FIVE: BUSINESSES, PROFESSIONALS, AND INDUSTRIES

HEALDSBURG'S STEAMBOAT. Yes, once upon a time Healdsburg was the proud but only temporary possessor of a perfectly good steamboat, during the long hot summer days in the year 1870, and this is how it all happened.

My mother and father both told about it when I was small. They were keeping company when it happened and were eye witnesses to the event. My mother was then a young lady of twenty, living with her mother and step-father, Lyman Dutcher, on the farm now owned by the Foppiano family, down the river road. Having verified the facts concerning this steamboat episode through other old-timers who lived in Healdsburg in those days, the story is as true as law and gospel. It came about as follows.

Back in the Devonin period of the town's history in the late '60s, a family named Hudson owned a pretentious ranch extending west from the river bank and south of the town, with a fine two-story house near the river, just above where the railroad bridge now spans that stream, only in those days there was no railroad, not even a county bridge. The old swimming hole of our youth, known as "Hudson's Hole," was just behind and below the house. It was deep and should have made a dandy place for steamboats to land.

The Hudson family were democrats and strong sympathizers of the southern confederacy, some of the boys were members of the KKK in Sonoma County, and I have heard my father tell that it was not healthy for an Abraham Lincoln man to talk freely, as most of the early settlers in the county at that time were southerners, many were fire eaters and blood thirsty.

The sight of a republican or a union supporter would give them a congestive chill. They would gnash their teeth, froth at the mouth, and were ready for a fight.

Anyway, the head of the house of Hudson was either a state senator or a representative in congress or something, and wielded great political influence, even after the close of the Civil War. Hudson was imbued with the idea that Russian River was a navigable stream and should be so declared by the powers at Washington and he had made so much noise on the subject, an effort was made to prove his theory.

Dr. and Mrs. J.S. Stone around 1928. (Courtesy Dr. Frank Wilson.)

True, in those days, the river was a far more imposing stream, the channel was a lot deeper, its breadth wider, the volume of water greater, as the mountain streams poured in much more water all summer so the scheme had some merit.

In the spring, perhaps it was April 1870, a steam tugboat was sent up the river, while the water was still high from winter rains, and succeeded in ascending as far as the bar just below where the dam is now located to retain water in Lake Sotoyome. She struck hard aground and fast, the water went down and left the tug high and dry on the bar and it had to be abandoned until the next high water when the fall rains set in, at which time she was repaired, re-caulked, and with the crew who brought her up the river the spring before, they sailed, or rather steamed, down the muddy water back to the sea, and the plan to prove Russian River a navigable stream was forever abandoned. So you all now know that Healdsburg once had a steamboat and if the river had only been more majestic, the town might have been a port of entry for foreign and domestic commerce. (To the late W.W. Ferguson, a good friend of a lifetime, the author is indebted for information contained in this story.)

SOME OLD TIME DOCS. Dr. Samuel Rupe was one of the pioneer physicians of Healdsburg and my good friend, Jerome Hobson, has ably told his story.

I did not know him personally, though my mother told me that he attended her when I made my advent into this vale of tears, June 2, 1872, in a small farmhouse on the old Dr. Cook place below the bridge across Russian River. I do remember very well, however, Dr. Forseman, Dr. Ely, and Dr. J.R. Swisher, who were in active practice when I was but a small boy. To me they were great men for they all wore voluminous beards and drove about with fast-stepping horses.

Dr. Lea, a lady physician, came to Healdsburg in the early '80s and for a time did quite some practice among women and children. Her brother was editor and publisher of one of the local papers, was a southern gentleman, a democrat, and was supposed to be related to the Lea family of Virginia. They did not tarry long but moved to other parts after a year or so.

Drs. Stone and Weaver, Dr. N.B. Coffman, and Dr. W.O. Wilcox all came to town sometime in the '80s and each and all did an average medical practice, being better than average medical men of their time. In fact they would tackle and do many heroic pieces of emergency surgery even out in the brush, getting fine results that would give the modern highly-trained medico a congestive chill or a spell of the jitters, for the modern medical man has to have the last word in everything with plenty of assistance, nurses, and ultra-modern equipment before he can work to advantage. Times and conditions have changed.

Once a man had a foot crushed under a locomotive wheel at the depot and was rushed up town to the undertaking firm of Grist and Young as there was no hospital within reach. Dr. Wilcox was called to operate on the man in the front window of the establishment, where all could see, for a large crowd had gathered on the old wooden sidewalk outside the window.

A local blacksmith administered the anesthetic (chloroform) and the undertakers acted as assistants. Dr. Wilcox rapidly and dexterously amputated the crushed foot while the curious crowd stood outside spell-bound, with faces glued to the glass, eyes and mouths open wide in wonder. When the foot was detached, all covered with blood, Dr. Wilcox picked it up by the toes and with a backhand stroke slapped it against the glass right in the face of a boy who was in the front line of spectators. It did not really slap him in the face, for the glass was between, but it might as well for he let out a blood-curdling shriek as the whole crowd fell back and several fainted on the sidewalk. The man made a good recovery.

Dr. Swisher told me of being called to the river bank below the bridge where some Indians had a camp in the willows. It seems there had been a family row and a buck had ripped his squaw's abdomen open with a sharp knife and her entrails were out and all covered with sand but not punctured. Dr. Swisher washed them off with warm water, replaced the many feet of intestines and with silk sutures closed her abdomen with through and through sutures. She made a good recovery and was about again in about a week's time, coming to his office to have the stitches removed.

In those wild and wooly days, most medical men could drink plenty of whiskey, gamble, ride or drive fiery horses, and tackle bare-handed and alone anything that came their way. Strange to say, most of their patients recovered and lived to tell the tale. Perhaps it was a case of "fools rushing in where angels feared to tread," or it may have been that we had a whole lot tougher citizens at that time, or perchance the medical men of that period more courageous than we moderns.

With all their foibles they were great men and did noble as well as heroic work. May their reward in the hereafter be greater than their recompence while here on earth. There were a few other medical men and women who came and went during my boyhood days but they did not impress themselves firmly upon the community.

PATENT MEDICINE SHOWS. They usually held forth each evening as long as the pickings were profitable on the street corner near the Healdsburg Bank, the site now occupied by the Bank of America. They always put on a good show to attract the crowd, which flocked to town from far and near, many coming from miles out of town; even staid and dignified members of the city's socially elite as well as financiers would pause to listen and get a laugh with the merry crowd at a funny song, a good joke, a slight-of-hand act, or an acrobatic stunt. Their spiels about the wonderful curative properties of their marvelous medicines were illuminating and convincing.

One fine looking fellow with a mustache like the horns of a Texas steer, a mane of wavy brown hair that hung to his shoulders, clad in a beaded buckskin coat, who claimed to be the Pawnee Indian Medicine company in person, having secured the formula for this panacea while living among the Pawnee Indians, would wind up his fluent remarks with this fine climax: "Ladies and gentlemen, this perfectly marvelous medicine is guaranteed to cure almost any disease to which human flesh is heir, from falling hair and dandruff to ingrowing toenails. It is composed of seventeen different kinds of roots, herbs, barks, buds, berries, and balsomes, culled from nature's laboratories, the fields and the forests, and all it costs is $1 a bottle; step up, step up, ladies and gentlemen, and get a bottle of this wonderful medicine, only $1 a bottle, six bottles for $5."

It was amazing how many perfectly sane and usually hard-headed people would cough up a $5 gold piece and proudly tote home a half-dozen bottles of "Tu-Ree" patent medicine, which was the supposed Indian name for this nostrum, to say nothing of dozens who purchased single bottles at $1 each.

Sometimes the spieler had an assistant to go through the crowd to sell to the more timid, who did not have the nerve to come up to the wagon in the glare of light. Why sometimes they would take in from $50 to $100 in an evening besides making sales privately from the headquarters in one of the hotels.

The Wizard Oil Co. was another gorgeous outfit that made regular trips to the old hometown and how they would unload hundreds of bottles of that precious product guaranteed to cure all pain and cure ague, it was good for sore throat, colds, cramp, colic, rheumatic joints, lame back, and a whole lot of other miseries. Their show was always good for many laughs and if the spieler could get the crowd in a good natured mood and laughing he could sell them anything and no limit.

This outfit, on one of their trips to town, had a stooge who would stand in the mob the first night and listen, mouth, eyes, and ears open in wonder, drinking in every word. On the next evening when a volunteer was called for to step forward to have the potency of Wizard Oil demonstrated on stiff joints and tense muscles, he would reluctantly come forward and show a badly ankylosed hand and forearm, one of the assistants who was a fine looking fellow would open a bottle of Wizard Oil before the eyes of the expectant crowd, have the man show his infirmity even letting doubting Thomas's in the audience try to open the hand and flex the wrist and elbow. Then when all were satisfied that the deformity was real the assistant would pour on a copious dose of the great life saver and briskly rub it in and keep on rubbing and manipulating until the stiffness began to relax when in a few minutes the poor man would be opening and closing his hand, moving it freely, much to his delight and the amazement of the gaping crowd. Of course they gave him the rest of the bottle for his own use, for he evidently was a poor man and how the sales mounted. Next evening he would be back to show what wonders had been accomplished and would fade from the picture, going to the next town where the process was repeated. It was a great psychological stunt and made the medicine more potent. Of course they changed stunts and stooges every time they came through the country, but the scheme always worked and the sales skyrocketed.

Another patent medicine vendor came to town selling a medicine to remove warts, corns, and bunions. One evening he was telling of the wonders of electricity and how Ben Franklin brought the lightning down from the cloud through a kite string and a key. As he talked he showed the audience a small battery and began unwinding a ball of twine. Then he passed out a loop of the twine and asked as many as could to take hold of it with both hands and form a circle; while he retained hold of the ends of the twine, some fifty or sixty boys and men took hold of the string while the man talked on the wonders of electricity and his corn, wart, and bunion cure. It was evident to those holding the string that he intended giving them an electric shock.

After they had held the string for some few minutes he paused and looked at the string holders as though astonished, just as though he had found something new and surprising, then he asked if anybody present knew what he had and as no one had a good answer or offered one, he laughed and said: "I'll tell you what I've got—the biggest string of suckers ever caught in this town," and the crowd roared with laughter and his sales pyramided, while warts, corns, and bunions disappeared.

One evening he told of a corn doctor who had a magic corn and wart cure, who received a testimonial from a grateful patient, which ran as follows: "Dear Sir: For years I have been troubled with warts on my face. I have used the bottle of corn and wart cure you so kindly sent me for $1.00. It is all and more than you claim for it, it worked fine. My face is all gone but the warts are still there. Yours Sincerely, Simon Green."

With such strategems and capers on the part of expert vendors of good, bad, and indifferent medicines, large quantities of medical junk were unloaded on an easily gullible public. Many other outfits came to town selling all kinds of things besides medicines but time and space forbid their enumeration or a description of their pranks for they, like many other features of the past, are almost forgotten.

THE HEALDSBURG TELEGRAPH AND CABLE CO.

It was back in the '80s that an epidemic of telegrapher's itch broke out among some of the girls and boys of the old hometown. It all started when Dellie Hassett and this historian conceived the plan to become expert telegraphers, so we borrowed two old telegraph instruments from Julius Alexander and with a coil of soft iron wire, insulators, a few old two by four timbers and some old-style crowfoot gravity batteries for basic materials, started work erecting the greatest telegraph line in the whole country. We hoped to outshine Western Union in due time.

A line was run from a pole atop our home, 20 Hayden Street to the belfry of the old N. Methodist Church and along up the alley on barns and poles to the Hassett home, also on Hayden Street. The instruments were hooked up, batteries and grounds connected, and it worked. Ecstatic joy was ours and the epidemic started. Other boys and girls took the fever and a line was run over to the home of Frank Gum, then a loop was put into the house of the Gaines family on Tucker Street and Caddie Gaines became a fan.

Next the line was extended downtown to the office of the *Healdsburg Enterprise*, edited and published by J.M. Alexander and C.B. Pond, both expert operators. A loop was run across Center Street to the Tom Hickey home, and he started his telegraphic career.

A little further down the street in a corner room of the city hall were the offices of Wells Fargo and the Western Union Telegraph Company, presided over by Harry Brown. Harry was a good operator and kind of liked Caddie Gaines. He had an extension run from the Hickey place to his office so he could chat by wire with the beautiful and charming Gaines girl.

We all had a lot of fun and were progressing wonderfully. Then C.B. Pond had a line run across several blocks to the Fried house so he could communicate with one of the

From left to right, Lizzie, John, and Mary Livernash, Ed Duncan, Florence Keene, and Ed Thompson stand in front of the Healdsburg Enterprise building on West Street on the Fourth of July, 1892.

older Fried sisters, who later became his bride and they lived in bliss ever after.

It was interesting to listen to the chattering instruments and read the gibberish going over the wire. Once in a while we could catch some sweet nothings passing back and forth when the operators thought they had the lines to themselves.

For a country town it was quite some telegraph line and before long all became expert at reading and sending messages in Morse code. The line was in operation for several years before it, like all other temporal things, disintegrated and crumbled into dust, or in this case, rust.

Occasionally a storm or some other accident would cause a break in the wire and would have to be repaired by the amateur linemen. Once several of the boys were repairing a break on top of the roof of the Albert Soules' house, corner of Center and Mill Streets. Dellie Hassett was on top of the roof and immediately tobogganed toward the eaves. The house was two stories high and the roof steep. There was no stopping place and no time to think. It was at least twenty feet to the ground.

Directly under him and over half way up the side of the house there grew, all spread out and receptive, a climbing rose, chuckful of thorns. The boy shot over the edge of the roof and went kerplunk into the sprawly, thorny vine and slowly by stages on down through the branches and briars to the ground. It was awful.

Of course the rose vine broke the force of his fall and saved him broken bones and perhaps his neck, but while it saved him other injuries, it did fill his clothes with rents and his skin with punctures and scratches. His face and hands looked as though someone had thrown an irate cat at him. He was a sight.

Dellie was a bit shaken and badly scared but very much alive. The rest of us stood by petrified, watching the catastrophe, breathed easier when we found he was not killed, and after applying good old tincture of arnica to his wounds, we resumed our labor. It was a close, close call, and none of us ever told our parents how Dellie got all scratched up for fear that an end would be put to all our fun.

BUSINESS VENTURE. The following story goes way back to the gold rush days, when the town of Healdsburg was a very small trading post, and was told to me by J.H. Curtiss, father of Thomas E. Curtiss and George Curtiss, in the '80s when working during summer vacation at the Curtiss ranch on the river road below the county bridge.

The story must be true for Curtiss was a deacon in the North Methodist Church and of course would not tell a neighbor boy a fairy tale. It seems that he and a friend came to California in the early days by sea, either around the "Horn" or via the Isthmus of Panama. On the way up the coast the ship was buffeted by storms that caused her to leak a bit and some of the cargo was damaged by salt water.

In the ship's hold was quite a consignment of chewing tobacco, which was in general use and a fashion of the day, cigarettes being almost unknown. Curtiss and his friend had some money between them and the friend had a bright idea, so when the ship reached San Francisco and discharged cargo the damaged portion would be sold for whatever it would bring. The two venturers in high finance purchased the lot of damaged tobacco for almost a song. Their plan was to dry it out, recondition and sell it at a profit, so the whole lot was moved out into the sand dunes to a spot near where the city hall now stands, the cases opened, the plugs removed and dried in the sun. As fast as they were dry the partners would brush the surfaces of the plugs over with a mixture of black lamp and molasses to restore its gloss and color, repack it in the dried out cases and before long had the whole lot in as good condition as ever and stored safely in a warehouse and ready for market.

Next thing was to find a buyer, for most anything would sell in those hectic days, so it was not long before a merchant from Sacramento purchased the whole lot at a fair bargain so far as he was concerned but at a substantial profit to the two speculators.

THE DRUGGISTS. Way back in the old days in the hometown there were drugstores as well as general stores, special stores, and saloons, the business interests and line of trade were well represented.

In those days there were two drug firms or, we might better say, apothecary shops who were more or less deadly enemies and hated rivals, no combinations in restraint of trade in that silurian era. Wright and Brown had a store in almost if not the same spot where the Brown Wolfe drug store now is located. Al Wright and H.K. Brown (known familiarly as Hank Brown) were the proprietors and they had a real old-fashioned drug store with colored bottles in the windows, old-style shop bottles on the shelves, with a mortar and pestle on a post at the edge of the sidewalk to tell the passing throng that here was a real drugstore where roots, yarbs, barks, powders, pills, confections, and elixirs were for sale to heal the aches, pains and ills of suffering humanity.

Al Wright was a fire eating republican, was something of a local politician, and could make quite an extemporaneous oration about the flag, the American eagle, and the glorious union whenever or wherever opportunity presented.

H.K. Brown, his partner, was rather tall, thin, had a beautiful flock of long billy goat whiskers hanging down from his chin, was a rabid democrat, and was a good influential citizen. He and his good wife lived on North Street and later built a house on Matheson Street where they lived for several years. They had a charming daughter Nellie, who taught in the local school until the great white plague marked her for the realms on high, and a son Harry who was a bit haremscarem and at one time was the local Wells Fargo agent and WUT Co. operator with place of business in the city hall until the same malady checked his baggage for life everlasting.

Wright and Brown sold to W.B. Whitney and he sold to Jones and Hobson (Jerome Hobson) who sold it back to Billy Whitney after a few years and so on to the present owners. Riley & Fox owned the rival store which was as up to date as could be at that time; in fact, they thought they were way ahead of all others in their line.

This store was sometimes known as the Red Front Drug Store, because the old brick building owned by Henry Fox had been painted a brilliant red.

Riley was a fine-looking Irishman, a Civil War veteran, a leader in local politics, a good druggist and citizen, and in addition to his charming wife he had a son, John A., now for the past forty years a practicing physician in Alameda, also a daughter, Maud, who was in my class in public school and was a favorite with most of the boys.

Dr. Mack Stone (left) and Rainey Haigh enjoy the view from the front of the W.R. Haigh Drug Store on West Street in the early 20th century. The Plaza Hotel was located next to the drug store. (Courtesy Edna Stone, Healdsburg Museum collection.)

Henry Fox, a small, dapper man, attended strictly to business and always made one dollar catch another, with a weather eye open for the welfare of Henry Fox. The Fox family lived in an ornamental old house with arbors, greenhouse, and garden at the corner of Center and Mill Streets. They had a daughter, Crystal by name, who was petite and the idol of her doting parents. Later another daughter was delivered by the stork express to make glad their hearts and fireside.

Sometime in the early '80s, Riley and Fox had a misunderstanding and Fox bought Riley out; then Riley opened another rival drug store in a room on the ground floor of the Sotoyome Hotel. Some years later he sold out and moved to San Jose.

In the early '80s another drug store came to town and opened up on the south side of the plaza and flourished for a time. It was owned and operated by Charles Weightman, a rather dressy fastidious fellow, a brother-in-law of Dr. F.M. Sponogle, who blew into Healdsburg about that time and whom I forgot to mention in the tale "Some Old Time Docs."

Dr. Sponogle was a big, wise, pompous man with skinny legs and a big fat tummy that looked like a balloon under his fancy vest. This pomposity, mental and corporeal, was supposed to add greatly to his professional dignity, although I doubt if it added to his professional skill. Dr. Sponogle did not remain long, but moved to San Francisco and Charles Weightman packed up his drug store, rags, bottles, and sacks, and moved to Oakland, where he remained until he went shouting home to glory.

My old school day pal, Rainey Haigh, had a pill shop in the burg for many years. He was a good friend and a mighty fine fellow. In the '90s there were two drug stores in town over a short period of time but they did not possess the vim, the fire, and the zeal of the old-time firms of Wright and Brown, and Riley and Fox, the two pioneer institutions. Back in those days, the local boys had a jingle which included some of the prominent people. It was as follows: "Fire! Fire! said Mrs. McGuire / Where? Where? said the widow Beck / Downtown said H.K. Brown / Heaven save us said sister Davis."

GUARDIANS OF OUR PEACE. This history sketch has to do with those brave men who by day and by night, in sunshine and darkness, in fair and foul weather, in winter and in summer, guarded the hometown folks and maintained law and order.

In the early '80s John Clack was city marshal. He was a good old-timer of medium size vertically but was quite thick, or may we say fat, in the region where he stored his daily bread. To help his walk he carried a heavy cane, and had an old British Bull-dog six-shooter in his hip pocket. He was a good town marshal, although if he had to run down a thief, it is more than likely he could not have overtaken a lame snail. He was a bit ponderous.

Of course, in those days there was little crime to deal with so his work was not strenuous. Most of his time was spent sitting about the plaza in the shade, displaying his badge of office, smoking strong cigars, chewing tobacco, and each evening at eight o'clock in the winter, and nine in the summer, he would ring the curfew bell hanging in the old tower in the center of the plaza and his day's work was done. Later the night watch rang the bell when he came on duty.

Following him came Ben Leard as guardian of our peace. He was rather tall and thin in comparison to his predecessor, wore a long tailed frock coat, wide-brimmed hat, carried a cane, a six-gun, and a pair of handcuffs. He was a good officer and tried to do his duty according to city ordinance and the Constitution. He was city marshal for many years and when he became a bit too old and decrepit for that post was made librarian of the public library. This library, when first started, was located in Prince's Hall and later, as it grew in volumes, was moved across Center Street to a large unoccupied room upstairs in the city hall.

The first night watchman to come within my observation was Richard Kinslow—everybody called him Dick. He was a good officer and always chased small boys home when they were out after curfew unless they were sent by their parents on an errand or were in company with an adult. Some of the larger boys resented his authority and would "sass" him back, but always they went home for they knew he would make good his word and lock them up in the city's Bastille.

One night in the late '80s the Healdsburg Cadets had a shindig, and after midnight in perfect formation, four abreast, the company started to march around the plaza. They had not gone far when Kinslow, his star ablaze on his breast and his night stick swinging, halted the parade and ordered them home. Most of the small boys in the rear ranks broke formation and beat it for home on the dead run, yours truly among them, for we all had a wholesome respect for the authority of our night officer. Some of the older boys tried to argue it out with him but law and order prevailed and they who remained on the firing line concluded discretion was the better part of valor and beat a dignified retreat to their respective homes. Once more the glory of yesteryears fades into the sunset to be forgotten, and thus another lesson in ancient history.

THE SAME OLD BULL. During the days of our innocent childhood in the '70s, '80s, and '90s, at regular intervals which allowed the stunned population to regain their senses and replenish their depleted exchequers, there would arrive in the old hometown circuses with fake sideshows, patent medicine vendors with a great variety of cureall nostrums, soap peddlers who would wrap a $5 bill about a 10¢ cake of soap, replace the original wrapper, and seemingly drop it into a pile or row of similar cakes, stir them up and glibly offer the crowd a chance to pick out the lucky cake for $1 and how the deluded onlookers would fall for the trap and part with their dough.

It was all trick and device, subterfuge and sleight of hand, for only about one in fifty would get the coveted prize, though hundreds bit at the slick talk of the verbal gymnast. Gadgets and baubles of all sorts would be offered for sale, sleight-of-hand artists, tight-rope walkers, slickers with shell and pea games, three-card monte, and other catch-penny deadfalls to skin the public and fill their coffers, came and went in large numbers.

These were the gangs who passed out the bull, blatantly, over-awed the juveniles, impressed the adults profoundly, made a cleanup and moved on to other green pastures before the deluded populace woke to the fact that they had been swindled. Many times as a small boy I stood at a respectful distance and drank in the fluent flow of oratory by these mendicants holding forth at a corner of the dear old plaza, as they hoodwinked, bamboozled, and deluded the gullible members of the body politic.

These men and a few women looked well, dressed well, some in silk toppers and frock coats, some as cowboys with gaudy outfits, others as Indian chiefs in feathers, beads, and buckskin, and still others as frontiersmen in buckskins with fringe, their hair long, even sweeping their shoulders; and lest we forget, even the Seven Southerland Sisters with gorgeous braids of luxuriant hair reaching to below their knees. How their spielers could bark with their barker's spiel. This was all before the days of modern science, pure food and drug laws, uplift by the dear sobsisters, and relief for the fat, lame, and lazy.

Those were the glorious care-free easy-going days when every man and woman killed his own snakes and all were happy in their ignorant simplicity, even the children, the overaged, and the morons. Today we have all kinds of laws regulating our lives and actions, laws against the bilk and bunk, unfair this and that; you must do thus and so; food fads, health cranks, vitamins, psychiatrists, and what-not, and while everything is simon pure, open, and above board, we the people are getting an eye and earful of the same old bull more elegantly and cleverly disguised.

Our mail is loaded with misleading junk, insidious propaganda is cunningly disseminated, foxy advertising fills some of the daily press and magazines, many commercial broadcasts over the air pour forth craftily worded boosts for worthless trash and unnecessary junk, our beautiful countryside scenery and buildings are smeared with hideous signboards, blatant by day, illuminated by night (up to dimout time), and it all boils down to the same old bull, only garbed in more subtle attire, flowing smoothly from honeyed tongues or fabricated by pen or brush.

The Children of Israel gave Moses the jitters when they worshiped the golden calf; other ancient peoples did and still do adore the bull; we moderns all still love the same old bull, and thus endeth another lesson in and comparison of ancient, medieval, and modern history.

THE LIVERY STABLES. Back in the days of our youth and long before, in those historic, glamorous horse-and-buggy days when six miles an hour was considered good average speed, livery stables flourished and were a definite feature of the life of the period. Fact is that many cities of that time enacted laws limiting speed within the city limits to six miles per hour and occasionally arrests and convictions took place even in the old hometown.

Healdsburg had its share of those wonderful institutions. Some bore names such as "The Geyser Stables," "The Sotoyome Stables," "The Fashion Stables," etc. Three were located almost in the heart of the business section; one over across the slough near the celebrated Kentucky Saloon was owned by Jesse King, and the last in the list was started by Ed Bale, being located on Fitch Street, near Tucker.

Among the early proprietors of stables we find William Cummings, Jesse King, N.W. Bostwick, William Brice, John Edrington, Lew Helman, and later on J. Connor, Tom Neely, Frank Newland, Jimmie Guerin, and Jerome Hobson. They all had fine horses, snappy rigs, showy harness, and other gaudy trappings, all of which were kept shining like new. You could hire single, double, or four-horse outfits all the way from carts, open buggies, and carriages to carryalls and buses.

Each proprietor took pride in the perfection and appearance of his stock and equipment and how elated the local boys would be to have the pleasure of taking the lady of their choice out for a drive in the evening or in the moonlight or for a long drive on Sundays behind high-headed, high-stepping speedy horses in gorgeous rigs.

For many years a six-horse stage driven by John Edrington left the Geyser Stables each day for the resort of that name out beyond Geyser Peak. It was one of those old-time thoroughbraces of stagecoach days which rocked along, creaking and chuckling as it rolled onward behind the six prancing horses. With the picturesque driver, six ribbons and long whip in hand, everyone on the street stopped to look and admire—and John loved it, for he was a great reinsman. The Cummings Stable cared for and drove the Sotoyome Hotel bus to and from all passenger trains. They also drove the water wagon with which the dusty streets were sprinkled in the summer, drove the local hearse, and were headquarters for many of the locally-owned stallions.

During the breeding season each Saturday morning there would be a parade about the plaza of from ten to twenty of these fine big animals with a "Jack" owned by Mr. Rickman of the Mill Creek section bringing up the rear. The Cummings Stable had the

The Cummings Brothers Stable was located on West Street. (American Legion collection.)

only hack in town. This old hack could be used as an open or closed carriage and was used when celebrities came to town, or for funerals and on occasions to air for public gaze some underworld characters of gaudy plumage. The Brice Stables drove the bus for the Union Hotel and had its share of novelties. When any rigs went out from the stables for state occasions, the driver was decked out in a long black coat and high-topper to conform to the social dictates of the times.

George Warfield informs me that each Sunday when skies were blue his father hired a matched buckskin team from Jesse King to take the family out for air and recreation, sometimes going as far as Kellogg and back all in one day. This team was noted for speed, beauty, and endurance.

Now all these proprietors were fine men and outstanding figures in the life of the community, each doing his share toward its advancement. However, they employed a rather motley array of help as hostlers, drivers, and buggy and harness washers. Some were heavy drinkers and good for but little else, but the majority were real good fellows, some rather outstanding characters in one way or another.

A letter from Arthur Price calls attention to two rather outstanding characters who worked for the Connor stable. They were Ben Boyd and Bert Litton. Boyd was a Texan and looked the part, with a gigantic black mustache like the horns of a Texas steer. He always wore a large, pearl-gray Stetson hat which made the picture complete. He was always ready to fight at the drop of the hat and willing to drop it himself.

Bert Litton, a relative of the pioneer Litton family, had a charming wife who taught school in and about Healdsburg. In his own way, he was a bit eccentric. Another of these figures was Slade Capell, who drove for Cummings stable and worked for Proctor and Truitt at intervals as the notion took him.

The old horse-and-buggy days are gone, the livery stables are but memories, the moonlight rides in the long summer evenings are as pleasant dreams for the older generation to recall with a smile and so the march of progress is ever onward.

THE VILLAGE SMITHIES. Longfellow in his immortal "The Village Blacksmith" gives us a vivid and beautiful description of the time-honored blacksmith of that day in good old New England, but the smiths of our day were not all widowers. Perhaps only half of them attended church and sat among their boys, all of which is neither here nor there, for, by and large, they were all good men and true and we all are, or should be, proud of them.

The classic beauty of this masterpiece of American poetry was and is applicable to that great procession of workers in metals from the time of Tubalcain (Genesis, 4:22) all down through the ages to the present day. The ancients worshiped Thor and Vulcan; the hammer of the first and the forge of the second were symbols of might, right, and honesty. The armorers of the Dark or Middle ages were held in high esteem by kings, princes, and potentates for their skill with hammer and anvil and for the beautiful work they produced in the way of weapons of offense and defense, many of which have been handed down to us as works of art.

What would our race be today without that long line of powerful men who wielded the hammer and forged the metals all through the ages past?

Healdsburg had its galaxy of noble smiths from its very foundation; for shortly after Harmon Heald opened his trading post in 1852, a man by the name of Morse arrived by team with necessary equipment and opened a blacksmith shop in a building he erected on the site later occupied by the Sam Meyer store. After a time Morse sold his business to William Dow and William Dodge, two honest smiths who proceeded to move their smithy to a location nearer the river hoping to start a rival town, but in this they failed, for not long after they moved, a man named Knaack erected a building and opened a shop on the very ground vacated by Dodge and Dow. William Dow was one of the men who played a horn in Healdsburg's first band in the late '60s.

Sometime in the early '60s, Mulgrew, a good honest Irishman, father of John, Felix, Cassie, Emma, and Josie Mulgrew, with his good wife and household goods moved into town and opened a shop on the corner where the city hall now stands; later this same shop was successively owned and operated by Lemoine, Tyler, and William Amesbury.

At times some of these men were partners, but when the city hall was to be built the old smoke-blackened building was demolished and passed into history.

John Marshall, father of Anabelle and Myrnie Marshall, had a shop for many years next to the livery stable on the corner of North and West Streets. As I remember, he wore a long black beard, which was the fashion in those simple days. He was a quiet man who worked from morning to night and kept his bellows blowing and his forge glowing year in and year out. After his demise a man named John Scott took over the business and carried on until the close of the blacksmith era.

The York brothers, Gus and Charles, had a smithy at the corner of Piper and West Streets. They were both big husky men typical of the village blacksmiths of the poem in many ways.

Over across the slough out beyond the Kentucky Saloon, Gus Lund had a shop in the good old days. F.I. Meyers, father of two charming daughters, one of whom, Alice, was in my class in school, owned and operated a shop on the west side of West Street, opposite of the old gristmill. This shop was successively operated by a Mr. Butler, later by Ed Phillips, and lastly by Sam Horton.

Andy Skillman, a local horse-shoer who worked at several of the shops, was an artist at his trade as well as a popular idol with most of the boys and young ladies. Nearly every owner of a fine horse wanted Andy to do the shoeing.

Many other traveling smiths and horseshoers came and worked and went their way during those long blissful years but few left any footprints upon the sands of time. A. Piatt and Sons had a carriage shop on Center Street across from Truitt's Theatre, but their work was confined to the building and repair of wheeled vehicles, although the ring of the hammer on anvil and steel made music day in and day out for many years at this hive of industry.

There is a thrill to be enjoyed listening to the cling clang, cling clang of the forge, the ring of steel on steel, and to watch the flying sparks from the burning coal or cherry red steel or red hot iron as the able smith welds or forges appliances for vital use or forms and calks shoes for a noble horse. Today but few of these old-time blacksmith shops remain, the garage and the auto repair shop have supplanted them in our modern economy but their memory lingers, a pleasant record in the hearts of we old-timers. And thus endeth another lesson in ancient history with a bit of a tribute of respect to the followers of Vulcan, the smith of the old Greeks. (To George Warfield, Arthur Price, and his brother Percy Price, I am indebted for some of the facts in this article.)

STAGE DRIVERS. In pioneer days following the creaking high-wheeled oxcart, the covered wagon, and horseback transportation, came the picturesque stagecoach and those glamor boys who drove them over all kinds of primitive roads, winter and summer, rain or shine, uphill and down, fording streams where bridges were missing, through ankle-deep mud in winter and clouds of dust in summer, carrying treasure, mail, express, passengers, and baggage.

They were affectionately referred to as "Knights of the Reins," for they were outstanding men among all the population of the wild and wooly west and were admired by all. The seat of honor on the stage was up in the box next to the driver. People fought for that honor; great dignitaries of state, glamorous ladies, and titled foreigners felt honored to be invited to occupy the seat of honor.

Mostly they were fine looking men, cool of head, steady of hand, clean strain, master of horses and of men, artists with reins and the long lashed whip. They dressed well in the resplendent garb of the day—high boots, doe-skin breeches, blue flannel shirt, pearl grey Stetson hat, and silk ban-dana. They could hold their liquor, could cuss fluently, if occasion demanded. They looked magnificent and were all perfect gentlemen.

Few of the old-time stage drivers packed a gun. It was up to the shotgun messenger, who rode atop the stage or sometimes inside, to do the fighting, although most of them were good shots with six-gun or Winchester. Their day has passed and the rising generation knows nothing of the gorgeous glory of a stage ride or the inspiring sight of a great Concord coach with four, six, or eight magnificent spirited horses, all resplendent in fine harness and the coach shining with paint. What a thrill! As they rolled over the road, the creaking of harness and the leather of the rockers instead of springs, the chuck and rattle of the wheels, the rhythmic pounding of the horses' hoofs, the occasional command of the driver, the crack of his long-lashed whip or the screech of brakes suddenly applied, made music that could be heard for miles.

It has been my good fortune to have known many of these outstanding men of Our Golden West. They were fine fellows, all in whom you could put your trust, but only a very few remain, the majority having figuratively made their last long drive over the long long trail into the portals of the past.

Some forty years ago, while practicing my profession in Copperopolis (now a ghost town) in Calaveras County, I knew an old-time stagecoach driver, James Borrell, familiarly called The Deacon, because he looked like a Methodist deacon and could steadily hold copious doses of nose paint. He drove stage out of Virginia City in the days of the Comstock boom. His outfit was a sixteen-passenger Concord Coach, with eight spirited western horses decked out with all the trappings of the day. He said that many were the trips of that same famed mining camp, and his coach would have one or two tons of 300-pound bars of bullion laid on planks in the bed of the stage, a full commitment of passengers, male and female, U.S. Mail, Wells Fargo treasure boxes, baggage, and a shotgun messenger atop the coach—and he had to make ten miles an hour.

The horses were changed at every station, which were never more than fifteen miles apart, usually every ten miles. That was some stage driving. On two occasions he had to stop the stage so that an expectant mother "taken short" on the ride, could give birth to a baby with the aid of other women passengers and the robes; while the stage, with the male element, went a piece up the road and waited for the blessed event to transpire. In both cases mothers and infants reached Sacramento in perfect condition, none the worse for their experience.

Sonoma County and Healdsburg had their share of illustrious reinsmen, who drove stage to and from adjacent towns and resorts before the days of modern transportation. A complete list is impossible but the following are well known, and a few are still in the land of the living.

89

Jim Miland, Jim Stewart, John Edrington, Chas. Foss Sr and Jr., Joe Downing, who was a tall, blonde, and handsome man, later a member of the San Francisco police force, Jim Higgins, Wade Hampton, Bob Mason, who for many years drove the four-horse stage from Skaggs Springs to Geyserville, two round trips a day for J.F. Mulgrew during the years that he ran that famous resort, Jo Sedgley of Cloverdale, who drove stage for years north from the end of rail, into Lake and Mendocino Counties and to the coast and the Geysers. His last run when quite an old man was into the Yosemite Valley.

Charles Vasser, also of Cloverdale, and still going strong, who drove stage to the Geysers for C.E. Humbert when he was in the livery business in that bubbling community.

The Ledford brothers, George and Irving, who for many years owned and drove a stage line from Cloverdale to Boonville and on to the coast town of Albion, they are still alive and both are driving autos instead of horses.

What with occasional holdups, unavoidable accidents, and, in some cases, inebriated or cranky passengers, our old-time stage drivers led hectic but gorgeous lives and to them and their traditions we moderns owe all honor and glory.

To F.M. Cooper of Santa Rosa, a grand old pioneer of Sonoma County, this narrator is indebted for some of the facts and names related.

Charles Foss Sr. was one of the first liverymen in Healdsburg. He could swing a coach and six horses in West Street, making a complete turn, horses on the run, without upsetting the stage, a feat of art if there ever was one.

Mrs. Robert M. McClelland and her sister, Miss Nell Sedgley, members of the S.C. Historical Society from Cloverdale, are descendants of Jo Sedgley.

Many of the stages mentioned here are preserved and on exhibition in the Willits Museum on Monroe Street.

THE SALOONS. Back in the good old days, long before the people of this country got bunked by the 18th Amendment, good whiskey sold in Healdsburg for 10¢ a glass and you could help yourself; beer was 5¢ for a large schooner; fancy drinks were unknown. Those hard-headed, hard-shelled, copper-riveted men of that day liked their firewater straight. In those days we had saloons, the prohibitionist and temperance fanatics calling them gin mills, grog shops, open doors to perdition and opprobrious names. There was sawdust on the floors, gaudy pictures and bright lights, women and infants under twenty-one were not allowed to enter their swinging doors. The average saloon keeper of that time held himself above such indecencies.

In looking over the list of the thirst emporia of the '80s and '90s, there was Rodie Gilbride, a good honest Irishman who ran the Oaklawn House and Bar down by the depot. There were oak trees about the place, but no lawn. He catered to the depot crowd and did quite a flourishing business because many citizens and railroad men had business at the railroad station and naturally became thirsty.

Out on the northern fringe of town across the slough there was Ed Pruitt's Kentucky Saloon. Next door was a deadfall which could be entered through his saloon. The women housed in this birdcage were about the ugliest old battleaxes one would want

Lads quench their thirst during an 1892 Fourth of July gathering in Healdsburg Plaza. Written on the back of the image is the following: "Everybody went to the celebration, so these poor guys made out they were having a good time." The writer was prudent enough not to identify anyone.

to see. Occasionally they would parade about the plaza in an open hack driven by Slade Capell for one of the livery stables.

Down in the heart of town Ike Gum and Al Zane had a bar at the corner of Matheson and West Streets. They were both family men, their wives and children attending Methodist Church along with the rest of us. King and O'Leary, two more good Irishmen, had a bar and wholesale liquor store about the middle of the block on West Street. The Union Hotel, run by Johnnie Grater, a German, and the Sotoyome Hotel, then owned by John Young, each had bars and catered to a fairly high-class trade.

Pat Lannan, another son of Erin, had a bar at the corner of Center and Powell Streets, where the Masonic Temple now stands. A man by the name of Barlow, who was short, fat, and asthmatic, and his wife who was a wonderful cook, supplied the hors de ouerves, which were appreciated by his clientele, and had a bar next door to the Farmers and Merchants Bank. He also prided himself on serving the elite of the city. J. Fried, a good honest German and his son Henry ran the Bank Exchange Bar, next door to the Healdsburg Bank on the spot now occupied by the Bank of America. Fried had two sons and three or four daughters. The daughters were noted for their good looks and were popular with all.

In those days we had five Irishmen, two Germans, some native-born Americans and one or two of the unknown racial strain, in the liquor business. Most of these men prided themselves on the high class of the good they offered to the public and frowned on the common drunk as a nuisance.

91

Card games, sometimes for high stakes, flourished in their back rooms, as at that time there were few so-called professional gamblers who inhabited the downtown section whenever there was a chance to make a cleanup, for gambling among some of the male element both in town and out in the country was a means of excitement. The local gamblers were not the gun toting, knife wielding, blood and thunder boys of the early west; they were smooth, polished gentlemen who took good care of themselves and did no manual labor. Some even, on occasion, attended church.

It takes all kinds of people to make a world. It is said that there is even honor among thieves, but when it comes to the old-time bar-keep of those bygone years, we have to admire them and say a good word for their deeds, their charities, and their efforts for the benefit of their community.

THE BUTCHERS. When a small boy, some sixty years ago, in the old hometown, we had two butcher shops—one on West Street, operated by Delano & Miller, the other on Powell Street conducted by Seawell & Moore. A little later on, a Mr. Markwell came to town and opened a shop in the Gobbi block on Center Street.

Those were pre-refrigeration days and, while they would have coolers packed with sawdust, ice was so expensive that it was almost out of the question, so the meat was hung about the shop on racks with big metal hooks, oftimes brought into the shop with the hide to facilitate the delivery of fresh, clean meat. Early in the morning, on cooler days, a few carcasses would be hung out in front so as to be seen by the passing throng. No screens, as in those days flies were considered harmless, so the little beggars buzzed about the meat, yet no one was made ill or died of food poisoning.

In addition to beef, pork, mutton, veal, and their by-products including sausages, occasionally deer, bear, quail, wild geese, ducks, cottontail rabbits, and even squirrels would be hung up and offered for sale to the public. Game laws were almost unknown in those days and seldom enforced. In those carefree prodigal days liver, brains, kidneys, and sweetbreads were given away. The butcher was glad to get rid of them, while whole hams and sides of bacon, sugar cured and smoked with real smoke, could be purchased for a few cents a pound, and were they good! I can still smell the fried ham, the ham gravy, the hot biscuits, or hotcakes, or corn bread, smeared with syrup or honey, along with a couple of fried eggs, a cup of coffee, and other good things that used to go with a breakfast of our childhood days.

From time to time, like all things in an ever-changing world, the personnel of butcher shops changes. Albert Soules, who at one time was part owner in the old flour mill, bought a half interest in the Delano shop when George Miller Sr. retired. George Jr. was at one time partner with Mr. Delano. The Markwells, after a few years, sold out to Delano & Soule; the whole family moved to Idaho, where they struck it rich in the mines.

Of course all butchers, like all grocerymen or farmers and everybody else, are perfectly honest most of the time, but they used to tell a story of one of the butchers, which may have some foundation in fact. When weighing meat on the old-fashioned scales, he would allow his hand to rest lightly on top of the meat, thus adding a bit to its weight. It was rumored that he had sold his hand so many times that it had made him rich. The story is a good one whether true or not.

Mr. Delano was a devout Methodist, Sunday school superintendent, and a Bible class leader; also he was strong with the Band of Hope, the Holiness Band, and any other collateral religious organization. He was profoundly religious but he did love, and drove, a good sporty horse in which he took great pride.

The firm of Seawell & Moore, in addition to being able and successful purveyors of meat and by-products, each had his family of one son and one daughter. The sons became outstanding medical men. The late Dr. J. Walter Seawell, who gave splendid service for many years in Healdsburg, and Dr. Will Moore, still carrying on an extensive practice in San Francisco, were both noble sons of noble sires. Both became good surgeons, for as small boys they had good examples of meat carving set by their parents in the slaughter house and butcher shops. The Delanos had no children. The Soules family had four or five as did the Markwells. There were several members of the Miller family, George Jr., Harry, and Emma.

There may have been other meat markets in the days before the '70s, but they were before my time, although back in those days many people did their own butchering and would either sell or give the spare meat to friends and neighbors. At that time meat was eaten three times a day; in fact most people had an idea that they couldn't live without it. What a difference there is between those care-free days of plenty and our present system of food rationing, with all the inconvenience, annoyance, and regulations we now submit to.

THE PHOTOGRAPHERS. When I was a small boy, along with a lot of other small boys and girls, our doting parents took us to the local photographer to have our cherubic features recorded, to be placed in the old family album along with those of bygone, and contemporary relatives and friends.

It was indeed a momentous event. After being posed rigidly with a metal support to steady our nodding noggins, and after the photographer had posed and reposed, adjusted and readjusted his camera under the black cloth, before shooting the picture, just to hold our childish attention he would hold his hand in the air, snap his fingers, and say, "Look at the little birdie." We innocent kids would look in vain for that rare avis and while looking, the picture would be shot. It was indeed an ordeal for parents, photographer, and the small subjects of artistic preservation.

Going back to the very earliest of history, when my mother arrived in Healdsburg in the spring of 1870, a photographer by the name of Alhands was holding forth without competition. What his initials were is lost in the dust of ages, but he was a fairly good photographer for the day and, on account of his odd name, was the butt of many jokes by the local boys, most of whom considered themselves pretty tough hombres.

Of course the town was growing numerically, financially, and artistically, so along about 1876 Andrew Price, another worthy follower of the photographic art, came to town intending to make a short stay, but he became interested in one of the Mulligan girls, who became Mrs. Price, and they settled down and lived in the old hometown for many years, rearing two fine sons, Percy and Arthur, who have both done well and are honors to the place of their birth and its public school system.

During those years the Geysers was a celebrated, fashionable resort where whole flocks of the rich, the elite, the great, and the would-be great congregated to show themselves off and make one another jealous. Andrew Price spent most of his time at this resort making good money taking pictures of these celebrities. The rest of the year he spent in town busily engaged in his chosen field of work. He was one of Healdsburg's well-known and beloved citizens, remaining until 1900, when he and his family moved to Berkeley.

Along in the '80s the Piatt family moved to town. One member of this large family, C.E. Piatt, was a photographer, and for a number of years conducted a gallery where people went to have their youth and beauty recorded for future generations to admire. Itinerant photographers would come and go, some conducting their business in tents, others in buildings, seldom remaining more than two or three months at a time, being what you might call gypsy photographers.

In looking over my collection of old photographs, I find many bearing the names of Alhands, Price, and Piatt. These three seem to be the only ones that were stable, possessed families, and became definite parts of the body politic. Alhands, being a green Easterner when he came to Healdsburg, was initiated by the boys, who took him snipe hunting and played other practical jokes. Andrew Price was a rather serious man with good intentions and never the butt of early day horse-play. C.E. Piatt was a devout Methodist and of course refrained from the sins of the world during all the years he resided in our midst. To these able men and their good work, we who survive owe a debt of gratitude.

Six: Religion

THE DAYS OF CANRIGHT. It was in those dear old peaceful horse-and-buggy days of the mid-'80s that Elder Canright blew into Healdsburg with a burning desire to debate the question of which day of the week should be set aside as a day of rest and worship. Elder Canright had been a very active leader, teacher, and preacher in the Adventist faith who followed the Jewish custom of worshiping their great Creator on Saturday, the seventh day of the week.

Due to some misunderstanding with the big guns in his own church he had broken loose from the fold and gone over to the other side who served their maker on Sunday, the first day of the week lock, stock, and barrel. Such little misunderstandings through past ages have made many crusaders and dissenters in religion, medicine, philosophy, politics, and ethics. Elder Canright was tall, gaunt, with a long honest face like a horse, with a sonorous voice that carried conviction as to the purity and zeal of his intentions. He was a born fighter and would throw his whole soul into any cause he might espouse. He contacted all the pastors of the other churches including Father John Meiler of the Catholic Church and convinced them to back his play and he would issue a challenge to the leaders of the Adventist Church to debate the question of biblical authority as to which was the proper day to observe.

The challenge was accepted, Truitt's Theater was engaged for a five-day session, hundreds of extra seats were installed to make room for the vast throngs who would attend, and did they come from far and wide, from all the flocks by the hundreds. From the start the old theater was filled to capacity, with hundreds standing who could not find seats, some even brought seats with them; interest and excitement ran high, everybody was up on their toes, a great verbal battle was fought. Each evening's debate was opened with prayer and closed with a benediction as all properly conducted religious services should be, and while it lasted, it created more interest and enthusiasm than any other thing that had transpired in the old hometown.

I can remember to this day the majestic appearance Father Meiler made as he pronounced a beautiful benediction at the close of the first evening meeting; later he and his followers withdrew from the the meetings due to some casual remark by a pastor of one of the other churches which Father Meiler did not like. All other attractions and activities were forgotten, for everybody, saint and sinner, young and old, rich and poor, great and small attended these meetings and were held spellbound by the flow of oratory by both sides, for great guns from the Adventist side were imported to offset the logic, power, and fervor of Elder Canright.

It was a great verbal battle, and after it was all over and the bills paid by freewill offerings taken up each evening, each side was more firmly convinced than before that their particular day of rest was the right and proper one ordained by God on which to offer up the devotion to "Him who holds the Universe in the Hollow of His Hand."

Elder Canright pocketed the surplus funds as his share, for "Is not the laborer worthy of his hire," and departed to greener pastures. the *Healdsburg Enterprise*, then edited by J.M. Alexander and C.B. Pond, in its issue the week following commented on the great debate and suggested that the people of Healdsburg discard the old calender and begin dating time from Canright. Thus endeth another lesson in ancient history.

My First Sunday School Teacher.
Shortly after moving to Healdsburg in the spring of 1880, my mother started taking her family, consisting of my two small sisters and myself, to Sunday school at the old Methodist Episcopal Church (North), and I was placed in a class of small boys with Mrs. Susan B. Currier as teacher. In those days the Civil War was still being fought verbally, and many of the Protestant Churches were divided into northern and southern branches, each branch thoroughly abhorring the other, yet devoutly worshipping the same God.

Mrs. Currier was a widow lady, well along the pathway of life, and she was an old dear. She believed every word of the bible as law and gospel, along with hell fire, eternal damnation, and Heaven with gates of pearl, streets of gold, harps, crowns, and snow white robes, without a doubt in her mind and tried to live according to the teachings of the "good book" and the North Methodist Church.

She never missed a Sunday at church, a Wednesday night prayer meeting, the Band of Hope, the Epworth League, a ladies aid, or church social. She was always the first to arrive, and the last to depart. Once when asked why she was so faithful, she answered by saying, "It is my duty and if I never miss a meeting, and am the first to come and the last to go, no one can talk about me behind my back." Even in those devout days the dear sisters of the church used to criticize one another a bit in spite of the Seventh Commandment.

There were, as near as I can remember, the following boys in her class: Will Zane, Frank Gum, Dellie Hassett, George Curtiss, Will Pride, Lester Gale, Bert Soules, and myself. We were all good little boys and obeyed our dear teacher most of the time.

After the general opening service she would start her class work by a series of questions, each in turn being catechized about as follows: "Now Willie Zane, have you been a good boy this past week, have not said any bad words, have not smoked any cigarettes, have not told any lies, have not disobeyed your papa or your mama, have said your prayers every night?"—to all of which each in turn would solemnly answer "yes." On rare occasions some boy would admit an infraction of her rules and instead of scolding, she would look sorrowful, praise him for his honesty, admonish him not to do

Much of daily life in Healdsburg and other small communities centered around religion and church activities. Tom Young, Evert Porter, Albert Garrett, Hiram Holcome, and Fred Beck drew inspiration from Sunday school classes at the Presbyterian Church in the late 19th century.

so again, telling him she was grieved, but to try and do better in the future. After this each would recite a bible verse from the card given him the Sunday before, then she would discourse to us upon the lesson of that day, and wind up by telling us we were good little boys and would give each a small card with the word "good" printed on one side and a verse from the bible on the other. When we had received a specified number of these "good" cards and had memorized the verses, we were given in exchange a large and more beautiful card, which we could keep as a reward for having been good little boys.

This dear old lady took a great deal of interest in our well-being, would come to see us if we were sick, and each Christmas would have a small present on the Sunday school Christmas tree for the members of her class. Of course we all chipped in and put something on the tree for her, and no matter what it was, her joy was unbounded and we were made happy. There was no question but that she exerted a good influence over the young lads in her class, and while at times we all may have thought her a bit exacting, we all loved and respected her for her many kindnesses and good deeds.

She passed to her eternal reward many years ago, and if there is a Heaven with gates of pearl, streets of gold, etc., she is clad in a white robe, wearing a crown, and perhaps playing a harp before the great white throne, happy through all eternity, as a reward for a well spent and useful life, which she richly deserved.

"LET US GATHER AT THE RIVER." It was way back in the gay '80s and '90s, usually in the month of April when there was plenty of water in the river and at times even a bit muddy, that large crowds would gather at the river to witness the ceremony of baptism. Every winter nearly all the churches held revivals or protracted meetings as they were sometimes called and at the close there would be a goodly flock of the saved to receive the rite of baptism and have their sins washed away before being gathered into the fold.

Some churches believed in sprinkling while others held to the tenet that immersion was the only proper way to be prepared for eternity and it was these baptismal services at the river that brought out the crowd. A pool below the county bridge opposite the home of J.H. Curtiss, where the water was sufficiently deep and the current not too swift, was the usually selected spot. When a baptism was to take place on a Sunday it was a great drawing card for the devout as well as the idle curious to congregate in large numbers, the devout on the west side of the river and the sinners on the eastern shore.

The baptismal party would usually erect two tents back toward the willows where those who had been immersed in the cold water might change their clothes so as not to catch their death of cold. The congregation would sing a hymn or two appropriate to the occasion, the minister would offer a prayer, then all dressed up in his best Sunday-go-a-meeting clothes he would wade out in the river to gauge its depth and make sure of his footing.

One by one the candidates for a better life would be led out and with solemn ceremony plunged under the flood and returned to the shore and the arms of loving friends to be comforted while the rest of the dear brothers and sisters would lift up their souls in a fervent song, usually one of those grand old hymns from the Gospel Hymns.

The newly baptized brothers usually took the service with more or less calm dignity but now and then a more emotional dear sister would give a scream as she was lowered into the icy water and come up coughing, choking, a bit hysterical but always crying; to shed tears was a fitting and proper way to express emotion and show the world that a deep and lasting impression had been made.

On one occasion a slender and callow young preacher was to baptize a rather large and weighty young sister, the congregation was singing "Throw out the life line, someone is sinking today," and just as she was about to be immersed she became panicky, screamed, threw her arms about her pastors neck and they both submerged together, there was a splashing and floundering about in the water when two stalwart elders with presence of mind rushed to the rescue, the pastor, the dear sister, and all were safely conducted to the shore, all-be-it a bit shaken. It was the hope of seeing some such event that caused the large crowds of sinners and idle curious to gather at the river.

THERE'S STILL MORE TO FOLLOW. When a small boy with my parents attending the different kinds of services at the old North Methodist Church, we had Sunday school, church, class meetings after regular service, young people's meeting, later known as Christian Endeavor; in winter they had revival, or, as they were sometimes called, protracted meeting, and we kids were always profoundly impressed. Somehow we did not attend Wednesday night prayer meetings, although my grandmother did, being very devout.

Revival services especially affected me, being of a rather emotional temperament, for when I listened to the great preacher or revivalist rant and rave about the sins of the world and appealed to sinners to forsake their evil ways and come forward to the Mourners bench and be saved, I usually went along with the rest and could almost see the gates of Hades opening to receive my sinful soul, and fancied I could smell the sulphurous fumes rising from the bottomless pit. Many other boys were similarly affected, and we would all weep and rejoice together, and vow to live better lives. But when the revival services were over, and spring and summer came with all their temptations, we usually got over religion and backslid into sinful ways.

Even at these solemn services, amusing events took place to lighten the burden of our sins. On one occasion, class meeting was in progress and as usual the participants waited for the spirit to move them; one would pray, others would give testimony, and someone else might start one of those grand old stirring hymns, such as "Rock of Ages," "Let Us Gather at the River," "Revive Us Again," or some other of those beautiful songs that will stir and sway the hearts of men for ages. Great and solemn was the religious fervor engendered at those class meetings.

On this particular occasion the usual service had progressed satisfactorily when there came one of those long oppressive silences in which the spirit failed to move. Now,

99

among the congregation this beautiful Sunday, occupying a whole pew, sat a dear brother, his wife, and their six children, one on either side, while he held in his arms the next to the youngest child. His good wife had the younger one, about a year old, asleep on her lap, while that blessed bird, the stork, was hovering not far away for the seventh time.

The silence was becoming oppressive when the dear brother started that grand old hymn, "Still There's More To Follow." He evidently took literally that Biblical injunction of "Be ye fruitful and multiply and replenish the earth." Most of the congregation, including the minister, smiled, some even tittered behind their hands, handkerchiefs, or fans. The dear brother, not knowing what occasioned the mirth, sang on fervently, and one by one the whole congregation joined in and were singing with all the power at their command. No doubt this supplication to Heaven was answered for year by year other members were added to the dear brother's family.

SHAM BATTLE. During the pastorate of the Rev. A.T. Needham in the '80s at the old North Methodist Church, then located at corner of Sheridan and Hayden Streets, about two blocks from the depot, the California National Guard held several summer camps at Seamans Pasture, so called although the property belonged to the Matheson family.

The Rev. Needham was a good man and true, and following the teaching of the Good Book for he was the father of a family of five boys ranging in age from five to fifteen years of age; they were more or less full of the old nick and mischief as the sons of ministers should be, according to tradition. Each year during the encampment the state troops would put on a sham battle which, to the small boys on the sidelines, was a soul-stirring and thrilling event.

Dellie Hassett, a son of Charley Hassett, and a member of Mrs. Currier's Sunday school class, was my chum at that time and with the Needham boys we would frequently be in the lot behind the church. One fine day a Needham boy suggested we have a sham battle, which appealed to all, so we went en masse about a half block away to the Hassett place and gathered all the windfall apples we could carry as ammunition for our make-believe war. We returned to the lot taking strategic positions at either extremity of the same, the four Needham boys on one side and Dellie and myself at the other mighty army, each intent on the theoretic destruction of the other as we had learned the ancients did in bible days.

Our apple cannon balls, for this was to be an artillery duel at first before the final charge, were piled up as we had seen them pictured in the history books and an imitation bugle call sounded the call to open fire. For a few minutes the apples flew thick and fast without anyone scoring a hit, each boy was firing at will and without any definite plan of action, so the apples were easily dodged but they did crash with dull thuds against the rear wall of the church and the high board fence at the other side of the lot.

Dellie and I were outnumbered two to one although two of the Needham boys were only little fellows but they could throw apples, so we concluded to concentrate our fire on a definite target and both throw at the same boy, which was good strategy; if one missed the other was sure to make a hit, the plan worked beautifully. A volley was fired and one of the apples took an enemy trooper square on the nose with such force as to flatten the organ somewhat. The boy was so taken by surprise that he seemed transfixed and poised in the air with eyes protruding and staring into space, then he collapsed in a heap with nose bleeding from both nostrils and crying as though his heart would break. The unexpected success of this tactical maneuver and the sight of real blood so frightened all of us that as soon as we found the Needham boy was not killed we, i.e. both sides, beat a hasty retreat to our homes and the sham battle business so far as we were concerned was over for all time.

AN ANSWERED PRAYER. It was in the early '80s that the Rev. Gaffney was pastor of the North Methodist Church; an earnest worker in the service of his maker though not a brilliant preacher, he was slow—plodding but sure. He and his good wife were not young, she being some years his junior, but they did have two very beautiful daughters of school age and of course they attended the upper grades of the grammar school.

In those days both boys and girls attended school even into their twenties so the Gaffney girls were almost young ladies and admired by all the boys both in and out of the church. In addition to his labors with his own flock he would drive to Geyserville each Sunday after class meeting to hold divine services for the benefit of the good people of that community. At this period of our history times were rather hard for most of the people and the pastor's pay was meager; in fact, it was down to a bare existence even with the help of donation parties by the Ladies Aid.

It was getting along toward the end of the school term and the elder Gaffney girl was to graduate with honors and take part in the public exercises celebrating that momentous event. Sad to say she had no white dress in which to appear and the Gaffneys had no spare money with which to buy one; they were, figuratively speaking, up against a stone wall.

Mrs. Gaffney being a good Christian, believing in the power of prayer, secretly offered up a supplication to the ever living God that some means might provide for the purchase of a new dress for her daughter's graduation and this is what happened. On the Sunday before the exercises were to take place Mr. and Mrs. Gaffney were driving home from services in Geyserville, dust was several inches deep in the road, their hearts were a bit sad for the collections taken at both services were very small.

Dear sister Gaffney felt down deep in her heart that in some way her prayers would be answered and that the Lord would provide, so in silence she repeated her supplication to Heaven asking help to get the dress. As they drove along in silence her eye caught the gleam of some bright object in the dust, they had passed it before it dawned upon her that this might be the answer to her prayer, she asked her husband to stop the buggy; carefully she returned to a point beyond that where she had glimpsed the shining object and with greater caution retraced her steps intently scanning every inch of the road.

To her great surprise and joy she picked up a $20 gold piece from the dust in the middle of the road. Right there she bowed her head and offered thanks to the Giver of all Good for the blessings she had received. Of course both daughters had new white frocks for the close of school and who can say but that the prayers of this good woman were not answered.

How Sister Bess Was Scared.

It was in the year 1881 when the Reverend J.L. Maine was pastor of the North Methodist Church. He was a giant of a man, well over six feet in perfect proportion. He wore a full patriarchal beard of beautiful brown color and had very large hands with long and powerful fingers. He always wore a high silk topper and a very long black Prince Albert surtout with flowing skirts or tails; he was quite some figure to look at and in his way was a fairly good preacher.

He had the happy faculty of regularly visiting about among his congregation for the benefit of their temporal as well as their spiritual welfare and always tried to make friends with the children; would pick up every baby and small tot, bounce it on his knee or hold the infant aloft in his mighty right hand as though sitting in a chair, bounce them up and down, carrying on a lingo intended to delight them as well as to make himself solid with the fond mother. This pleasantry as near as memory serves me, was as follows: "titsy, watsy booby sucky, baby wanty dinner."

On one of his regular visits to our home he came in and found sister Bess, then about a year old, sitting on the floor playing with some toys, so to show his great love for children in general and sister Bess in particular he picked her up, tossed her into the air and caught her in his great right hand, bounced her up and down a few times as he recited his aforementioned jingle.

Well, it was more than any child could stand without being scared stiff and on this particular occasion Bess must have been badly frightened, even made panicky, for she lost control of her puckering string and baptized the reverend gentleman in a way he had never been baptized before—his hand and arm to his shoulder was sopped wet, even his face and beard was sprinkled.

Of course the family present were all horrified and shocked beyond expression except myself. I was delighted but could say nothing not even smile let alone have a good old hearty laugh at the preacher's discomfort, but it was my private opinion kept to myself that he was to blame and it served him darn good and right. Under my breath I felt like saying amen.

The Reverend Maine was a bit shocked at the suddenness of the deluge, put Bess down in a hurry, mopped himself with his handkerchief, admitted it was all his own fault and beat it for the parsonage to wash up and dry himself out for he sure had been rained on. Thus endeth another lesson in ancient history!

Church Socials.

In the days before cocktails, cigarettes, petting parties, road houses, equality of sexes, and relief for everybody but the men who really work, about the only form of diversion outside of Fourth of July celebrations, May Day picnics, and occasional circus, minstrel show, patent medicine outfit, or stock company barnstorming the country, was the good old-fashioned church social.

It was of many varieties, depending upon the season and the needs of the occasion. There were strawberry and ice cream festivals in May and June, harvest home or Halloween socials in the fall, then whenever they could and the church needed finances there would be others sandwiched in during the rest of the year.

As ice cream was expensive and rather rare in those days, it was considered a great treat and usually sold at 25¢ a plate with strawberries 10¢ extra; of course children were half price or 15¢. Sometimes these socials were held in the church, the parsonage, a private home, or when an extra large attendance was expected or a big dinner was to be served it was held in a vacant store in the business district.

And how a few of us boys would work, turning an old-fashioned ice cream freezer by main strength and awkwardness, hulling strawberries, running errands, collecting viands with an old horse and wagon, or going round and round the plaza ringing a bell and calling at the top of our voices, all about the social or dinner, its price and where it was to be held, and all this just for the pleasure of getting a free dish of ice cream with strawberries and cake or whatever was being served on that particular event. It was great fun and we all felt that we were doing things and going places.

The benefit socials were the ones that gave us quite a kick for nearly every member of the congregation came bringing gifts or donations for the poor pastor and his family as well as food to eat at the party. Some would bring useful things such as food, clothing, or household equipment which were good and worthwhile; a few brought that for which they had no use or need, such as fruit or vegetables they could not sell or use themselves, gnarly, crooked, or douty fire wood, or clothes no one would want.

On one occasion a dear sister brought a framed hand-worked motto "We Love Our Pastor," food for the soul but not for the body. It was the opinion of some of the boys that she had fished the old frame from the junk in her attic, yet the poor preacher had to accept all these things in a spirit of thankfulness and humility, smile and express gratitude to the donors, both great and small, for their bounteous kindness.

Of course we boys sized up the gifts and rated the religious fervor and purity of heart of the bestower by the quality of the gifts laid at the pastor's feet.

It was late in the '80s a great turkey dinner with all the fixings was given in a vacant store in the Gobbi block, which was well attended and all could eat their fill of good things, for second and third helpings were permitted. There was present at this dinner a local man who was both a physician and minister of the gospel, who was celebrated for his appetite and appreciation of good food and of course he ate his fill of all the good things on the table together with several helpings of turkey and stuffing. That night he was taken severely ill and proceeded to unload all his good dinner when something seemed to stick in his throat; he reached in his mouth and pulled out a long white object and in horror exclaimed "My God, what a worm," and soon recovered.

In eating large chunks of turkey he had swallowed a piece with about two feet of string used to hold the stuffing in the turkey's innards which he mistook for a worm. His good wife, thinking it a good joke, told a friend and so the story spread and for a time was the source of much hilarity.

Such events, like the dodo and other primordial forms of life have passed into oblivion and become cherished memories of our ignorant innocent youth. Thus endeth another lesson in ancient history.

THE REV. ANGUIN AND THE PIOUS DOG.

The following historical event transpired in the good old North Methodist Church sometime in the early '70s although I did not personally witness calamity, it having occurred before my time in this glorious county of ours, but I have heard my maternal grandmother tell it many times, chuckling with glee, her whole frame shaking and jellying with mirth, for she was a bit fat, it being in the days when no thought was taken of face or form excepting as nature provided.

The story must be true for grandmother was a devout Methodist of the old-time hard shell, shouting variety, abhorring the world, the flesh, and the devil and I know she would not prevaricate.

The Rev. John Anguin was pastor of the church at the time and in grandmother's opinion he was a very proper, Godly man, able and an efficient disciple of our Lord and Savior; far above the average rural preacher of his day, being a young man full of zeal just starting on a great mission with all the world before him. In later years he became quite a preacher in a big city church, being ambitious with a pleasing personality and could bring many penitent sinners weeping to the mourners' bench.

In the Sunday school each Sunday morning he taught a bible class of charming young ladies; this was also in the days of flowing flounces before the advent of silk hose. It seemed that one of his flock who attended all of the many services had a little dog who was in the habit of keeping his master company and who devoutly attended church and Sunday school more or less as did Prinnie Pimm some ten years later.

Now the Rev. Anguin was an earnest, faithful Christian with a good kind heart who loved all the works of his Maker but did not believe that the House of God should be desecrated by a small dog so he made every effort to have the poor little religious dog kept home on Sunday. On this particular Sunday the little dog had eluded his master and succeeded in getting into the sanctuary he loved so well; the reverend gentleman was conducting a profound lesson in theology; all was well, peace and calm pervaded the church, when to his horror he discovered the little dog under a nearby pew; to think was to act, so taking his heavy cane he started to purge the House of God of the canine brute.

He took a swipe at the dog but only succeeded in causing the dog to emit a few yelps and change his position to beneath the pew in front of the class of young ladies. Again he reached under the pew and made a full arm stroke with his cane, the little dog being a wise dog filled with religious fervor, skipped out for a safer place behind the young ladies' feet and legs, to all of which the good pastor was ignorant as a new born babe so on his second swipe instead of dislodging the dog he took his young ladies a raking blow across their shins and they all went into the air with a scream, stark terror and surprise on their lovely faces.

This unforeseen turn of events somewhat flustrated the good man so he gave up the idea of excluding the little dog with religious tendencies from divine services.

He blushingly and haltingly apologized to the young ladies for his sad mistake and after order was restored to the Sunday school, for he sure had kicked up quite some commotion with the yelps and ki-yis of the dog, the shrieks of the young ladies with the battered legs and the laughter of all the rest of the Sunday school and teachers alike, so with great solemnity he continued the lesson about Lazarus at the rich man's gate whose sores were licked by the dogs of the street. Thus endeth another lesson in ancient history.

THE NORTH METHODIST CHURCH. Looking back through the colonades of time with its beautiful arches depicting the successive stages in our onward progress, to the rosy mists of boyhood days in the old hometown when life was just one long sweet song and the real trials of modern existence were unknown, we occasionally think of outstanding features and events that transpired.

The choir of the North Methodist Church was one of these features and here follows a few facts concerning that changing yet ever living institution. Shortly after returning to Healdsburg to live in 1880, my mother, who was quite a singer for that time, joined the choir. Who the other persons were that composed it at the time have been forgotten, but before long, W.N. Gladden, who lived on a fine ranch down the river road and for a time in the '70s operated an old-fashioned gristmill back of Powell's Opera House, with its frontage on West Street between Matheson and Mill Streets, became leader and first tenor.

Mrs. Joy and her eldest daughter Effie were also members, my father was basso, and Mrs. I.A. Delano was organist. When the family of Henry Alexander came to town, Louis and Frank, his elder sons, having fine voices were pressed into service, the first as tenor and the second as basso profundo, to make the double quartette complete. Mrs. Bowsher entered the choir as an alto with Mrs. Joy.

This choir had a reputation for well-blended voices and good music, so each Sunday evening for a half hour before the regular devotional exercises a praise service would be sung at which time the choir would lead the congregation in singing and would render one or two special numbers for the pleasure and edification of those present.

To me there is nothing grander or more inspiring in the way of music than to listen to a good choir leading a congregation in singing selections from that old standby, "The Gospel Hymnal" as though they were pouring out their very souls in praise to the Most High; it makes a deep impression.

The M.E. choir in those days sang well and the church would be well filled with the devout and the worldly, the latter came to enjoy the music, for there were no movies, night clubs, cocktail bars, or road houses to detract, so they went to church. Of course changes came in the personnel of the choir, the Alexanders and the Joys moved away. Mrs. Frank Cummings sang with them for a time and Amos Stanger, a fine basso, came to town and added his voice to soulful song.

John Gunn and P.J. Ferguson also were members of this choir at different times, as well as several ladies whose names have been erased by time.

105

The Methodist Church at the corner of Fitch and Hayden Streets. (Courtesy Jack Relyea, Healdsburg Museum collection.)

On special occasions they would augment the regular choir with a whole flock of larger girls and boys from the Sunday school. It was thrilling to sit up on either side of the adult singers, look out over the congregation, and do our best to intensify the volume of sweet sonorous cadences, even though some of the boys had no ear for music and could only growl along on two bass notes, sometimes in tune and sometimes off key. Fortunately those feeble discords were drowned in the mass of melody.

Every Friday evening was choir practice and it was great fun for some of the younger members of these families to be permitted to attend as spectators. In the good old summer time these rehearsals were held in the church; in winter when storms beat and the wind howled they were held at our home where all was warm and cozy. We would watch the singers line up in proper order, Mrs. Delano at the piano or organ with Gladden in a position where all could see him. He would, with small baton or his right hand, index finger extended as straight as a crooked finger could be, beat the time as he conducted the choir. They would go over each passage with minute care, sometimes repeating them many times until he was satisfied it was just right.

In carrying out his instructions at these practices he would use such words as forte, fortissimo, piano, pianissimo, crescendo, adagio, andante, diminuendo, etc. as was indicated by the score. He was a great stickler for all these shades of tone and time and when the choir was singing in public he made signs with hand or baton as he beat the time, conveying the meaning of the aforesaid musical terms to the singers he directed.

They used to tell a joke on Gladden. It seems that when Patti came to San Francisco on one of her grand tours, Gladden went down to hear her and was fortunate enough to get a front seat in the middle of the first balcony of the old opera house where she was to sing. When the diva appeared and thrilled the vast audience with her flute-like voice, Gladden leaned well out over the balcony rail, his face beaming with ecstatic joy as he turned his head from side to side so as not to miss one sweet note of the singer's voice. Reflexively he beat time as a matter of habit. He would do the same thing when the band played. Some other Healdsburger was present, observed and told the story so his friends had a lot of fun twitting him about beating time for the great Patti.

There were other good singers and choirs in Healdsburg during those days but to me the old M.E. choir was the outstanding feature, my father and my mother both sang in it, mother for over ten years, and in fancy she is visible and her voice is still heard.

THE ROW IN THE CHURCH. From the beginning of the invention of music by Jubal, Genesis, 4th chapter and 21st verse, varying degrees of melody have served man from that of extreme piety to the depths of degradation.

As man's singing gave expression to the soul and helped in the rendering of due homage to the God of our fathers, or even to the worship of the heathen idols early in the history of the race, it became a part of all devotional services. Jubal played the harp and organ, David the harp, Pan had his pipes, and many others had the lyre, the lute, and the horn as musical instruments, and so on down through the ages.

But the old-timers who believed in a simple, fundamental religion without show or ostentation banned all musical instruments from devotional services as the work of the devil. As many of these old-timers could not read, and hymn books were scarce, congregational singing was the vogue. The pastor would read a line or two of the hymn and all would join the singing, following the lead of someone who was better versed in psalmody.

This was the custom in services of some churches in Healdsburg, even when I was a small boy. Sometimes the pastor would read a whole verse or even the whole hymn through before the worshipers took up the air and sang with all the fervor of their beings. It was grand, inspiring music, and no doubt echoed to the very gates of Heaven.

In north Healdsburg, not far from the main highway on a wooded knoll, stood a plain white church known in those days as the Campbellite Church. The congregation was fairly large and very devout in their simple way. It shunned all modern innovations as unholy. However, there was a younger and growing faction in the church which believed in keeping pace with the times and suggested that a melodeon be purchased and a choir organized. (These little melodeons were the forerunners of the church organs; I can recall my parents having one.)

This plan had the quiet approval of the Reverend Albert G. Burnett, who was pastor of the church at that time. He was quite progressive, for he progressed from preaching to teaching, to the Sonoma County Bar, then to the office of district attorney, next to be judge of the superior court, and lastly, to the appellate bench of the state. He was able and up-to-date, but did not dare come out openly for either side in the church row, being a good politician, between the lined hymn singing and the more modern choir-led singing factions, supported by an honest old melodeon, and all to the glory of God.

So the moderns on the quiet organized a choir, purchased a melodeon, and began practicing in the home of one of the members and started to talk up the modern trend in Sunday services. Of course, the old "hard-shell, die-hards" would not listen to such a desecration of the house of God, and made it known that if any musical instruments entered the church, they would leave. And it so happened when the melodeon, and the choir, did come into the church, the old mossbacks left in high dudgeon. Some went to other churches, some remained at home, and in the privacy of their own closets, did reverence to their Maker. For a while, the battle between the factions raged fiercely and threatened to wreck the church, but as time went on and the church was not smitten by the wrath of the Almighty, one by one and family by family many came back into the fold and the church moved onward and upward to greater glory.

Be it known, however, there were a few so set in their doctrines and dogmas that they never again attended a modern church. Thus passed without severe damage a doctrinal dispute, but it took a long time to heal the figurative wounds. (To my good friend, W.W. Ferguson, now deceased, whose parents attended this church at that time, I am indebted for some of the facts, although as a small boy, this little scrap was frequently spoken of in the hometown.)

ONE ON GRANDMA. In those days when this recorder of events was a very small boy and ladies who considered themselves in style wore many feathers as decorations on their bonnets, rooster feathers were quite popular. Some wore them as nature made them in natural tints and hues; others had them dyed gaudy colors, and some wore them black. They were all beautiful in a primitive barnyard sort of way.

The following tragedy happened to my maternal grandmother, Mrs. C.E. Dutcher, one Sunday morning while attending divine services in the old North Methodist Church which was not far from our home—perhaps it was in '81 or '82. Grandmother was in deep mourning, having lost her second husband, Lyman Dutcher, in the late '70s. Her first husband, Henry Schermerhorn, was killed in battle during the Civil War.

In those benighted days, widows wore their weeds very black and quite a while. In fact, many wore them until they concluded it was about time to shed their sorrows and look about for another man. To remain in deep mourning for a long time after the loss of a helpmate showed respect and was quite the rage among sorrowing widows.

Grandma dressed in deep black silk, carried a black-bordered handkerchief, wore a small black bonnet or toque (popular then), and for decoration had a whole flock of rooster feathers from a black minorca fastened at the back of her dainty lid in such a way that they curved forward over the front to give added grace and beauty to the ensemble.

On this particular beautiful Sunday morning there was to be a special service at the church, which most of the Sunday school kids would attend—it might have been communion service. Grandmother dolled herself up in her very best, for she was a proud old girl in spite of her religion, donned her feather-decked bonnet, and wended her way to the church, her heart filled with religious zeal. All the rest of the family had gone to Sunday school, so Grandma had to fix herself up all by her lonely.

Church services were about to begin, the congregation was seated, the organ playing softly, when Grandma, all decked out in her finery, wearing a black silk dolman embellished with long fringe and carrying a black lace fan, came regally into the church, occupied her pew, bowed her head, and silently offered up her devotion to the Ever Living God, as all good Christians of those days were supposed to do. Grandma was very devout; her religion was a very solemn affair. She believed every word in the Bible, including hell fire and damnation, the Ten Commandments and the Apostles' Creed, hook line and sinker. She was a sure-enough old-time shouting Methodist.

This dear old lady loved to attend all services of the church, Sunday school, class meeting, Wednesday night prayer meeting, and watch services held at the church the last night of the old year so that when the new year turned they could offer up their devotion to the Most High, asking His blessing upon the faithful throughout the coming year. Protracted meetings, revival meetings and, in the old days, camp meetings, deeply appealed to her sense of religious duty. She got a world of satisfaction out of her religious convictions.

To make a short story longer, when Grandma straightened up from her devotion, she heard someone titter behind her and, feeling in a solemn mood, turned to glower disapproval at the facetious party, for the church was no place for levity. Someone else giggled from the other side and grandma turned to awe this second disrespectful person with a frown. Others here and there about the church smiled or snickered or held their hands or handkerchiefs or fans to cover their grins or to stifle their merriment.

And so it went on, much to poor old grandmother's annoyance, for it kept her busy frowning this way and that. The ladies in the choir up behind the pulpit smiled, even the good man of God behind the Good Book noted what was awry and suppressed a grin, though there was a merry twinkle in his eyes.

Grandma sensed that all this disturbance had something to do with herself, but was at a loss to solve the problem, for she was always exact in everything she did. The word "error" was not in her vocabulary. She knew she was all "gotten up" in her very best, and thought herself about the proper caper for an elderly lady who had two dead husbands and was a good Methodist, so it bothered her, and was her face red! Yet she bravely stayed the service thru, joining in the hymns with all her soul and fervently saying amen with the rest of the worshippers. At last the service was over, the congregation began filing out of the church, some smiling and some laughing. It had been a joyous meeting. As soon as my mother could get from the choir, she rushed to grandmother and told the poor old lady that her hat was on backwards. It was so constructed that the feathers would flop up and down with the movements of her head when on backwards, but would behave properly when correctly placed.

This flopping of the rooster-tail feathers, plus the fact that the hat was on hind-sight foremost, gave the old lady a rather ludicrous appearance and when she scowled at the tickled members of the congregation the effect was more than a solemn service could hold in check, so they giggled right out in church, especially the younger ones. The old lady was a bit crestfallen, but being a good old spartan of puritan stock, gathered her feelings and good intentions that would get her into glory.

No doubt she has been there now these forty years, for her faith was implicit. She instantly quoted passages from scripture appropriate to the occasion and added that it made no difference with her Maker whether her hat was on the wrong way—her abiding faith, according to her stern code, was exemplary. May God rest her soul.

METHODIST TROUBLES, STORY NO. 1. When I was a small boy attending Sunday school and church in the old North Methodist Church, then located at the corner of Sheridan (Fitch) and Hayden Streets (now moved to Piper, near Fitch), grownups had doctrinal and other differences of opinion, even in the '80s. The Campbellites were not the only ones who had denominational troubles, as related in my story "A Row in the Church."

In those days the Methodist Conference used to assign pastors to the different churches in the circuit or conference, divisions of the state. Of course, the youngest and poorest preachers were usually sent to the smaller or financially depleted congregations. Seldom did the local church have any say about who should be their pastor. They took what was sent them. If he happened to please, they thanked God for the blessing. If he happened to be a ministerial flop, they thanked God he was no worse, for they had to put up with whoever was sent, for a whole year, and had to make the best of a bad situation.

Some divines felt that they had been called by the Most High to preach, as the following incident may illustrate. It seems that back in the good old days, a simple soul by the name of Walker got religion and felt the call to preach the gospel, but he wanted a sign from Heaven, so each day he went out into the woods to pray, hoping to receive a reply direct from above.

Each day he repeated these orations for some time without success. He was growing desperate and on one occasion he made a specially eloquent plea to the Great I Am, begging for that sign, for the fire to do good burned within him.

It so happened that on that very day a neighboring farmer had turned his mule out to pasture behind the woods and, when Walker reached the climax of his petition for a sign from Heaven, the mule, being lonely, lifted his head to the eternal blue and brayed. He seemed to say, "Wah, Wah, Walker, Walker; go preach, go preach." So Walker took it as an answer and went and preached, though he was a very poor preacher. No doubt many other preachers of the day received their call in similar fashion.

METHODIST TROUBLES, STORY NO. 2. During my callow years a few such pastors as described were sent to the good old North Methodist Church. One in particular was the Rev. Slaven, short in stature, broad of beam and deep of hold, with a gorgeous crop of black whiskers that came almost down to his waist line.

His good wife was about twice his size, good natured, easy-going, somewhat gelatinous, and admired delightedly everything her husband said and did. They had several small children about a year apart, who were little terrors. The Slavens believed in that Biblical injunction, "Be ye fruitful and multiply and replenish the earth," but not in that edict about sparing the rod and spoiling the child, so the members of the church got cold chills when sister Slaven made a call with her brood.

Bro. Slaven had a powerful voice and was emphatic in his efforts to preach soul-stirring sermons, as were many zealots in those good old camp meeting days. His pleading did not always delight his hearers and the congregation. They paid him his small stipend and made donations to help the divine keep the wolf from the fireside, but many stayed away from services, either remaining at home and praying in secret or by attending other places of worship.

Grandma Leard, mother of Ben Leard, occasionally attended services in the N.M. Church. She lived in a small house on Tucker Street about opposite the old grammar school, and one fine morning she passed from this transitory existenced to Life Everlasting and services were held for her remains in the N.M. Church, the Rev. Slaven officiating. He preached a very long-winded sermon eulogizing this dear old lady's many virtues and good deeds, all of which were true, doing his best to impress his hearers with his power, for the church was full of her many friends. Everybody loved this grand old Christian lady.

At the apex of his effort in oratory he told how "God came thundering up in the early morning hours with his big lumber-wagon and carried the soul of Grandma Leard away to Heaven." Well when his year was up the elders, deacons and congregation sent a letter to the presiding elder and one to the bishop of the conference asking that Bro. Slaven be sent to some other pastorate as they did not want him back in Healdsburg. The presiding elder, being a rather stiff necked and high-handed individual, insisted on his return, stating that Bro. Slaven had not been given a fair chance, that the brethren and sisters had not cooperated as they should have done.

Bro. Slaven sent a message expressing his delight, he would try to make amends for his sins of omission and commission, all would be well. But the church members had other ideas, so they got together and sent a message to the parties concerned refusing to receive Bro. Slaven back for another year, so the church had to do without a regular shepherd for quite some time, much to the joy of the kids and the distress of many of the members.

PREACHERS AND CHICKENS.

Way back in the days when the dictum "children should be seen and not heard," was in full force and operation, our family lived at 21 Hayden Street, not far from the spot where the old North Methodist Church was then located. In those happy days nearly every thrifty family kept at least one cow, had a flock of chickens with plenty of young roosters for the table, a garden, and a family orchard as a means of providing a goodly supply of provender in case of necessity, for company was liable to drop in at any time unexpected and had to be made welcome and partake of the choicest fruits of nature's storehouse, so it was necessary to have a well-stocked larder. My mother and her mother, known to us as Grandma Dutcher, were famous as good cooks and bountiful providers of appetizing dishes such as fried chicken, chicken with dumplings with lots of juicy gravy, corn bread, hot biscuits that melted in one's mouth, and many other good things that would start the flow of saliva, and so it happened that nearly every itinerant preacher or newly appointed pastor of the church came to our house on his arrival in town to have the inner man revived with large helpings of mother's good food.

Also in those glorious days children had to wait for the second table when special guests were present, which no doubt was proper for it was the custom. Also all preachers were supposed to be very fond of yellow legged chickens, especially when fried to a golden brown in new made butter, and from the way the average preacher or presiding elder could stow away all and sundry of the good things on the table it must have been true, for they could eat until they could only chew but could not swallow.

If their religious zeal was as great as their capacity for food and yellow legged chickens in particular, they surely ranked high with the Heavenly Host. My two sisters and I always resented the presence of such company for while there was always plenty for us to eat, the preacher usually consumed the best parts of the chickens and we had necks, backs, wings, and an occasional drumstick, parts we were not enthusiastic over, so in our childish ignorance a visitation by a pastor with a penchant for yellow legged chicken was a horror rather than a blessing. Being dutiful children we curbed our feelings, suffered in silence although we frequently thought damn or words to that effect. Any way we were always delighted when the preacher departed and life resumed the even tenor of its ways.

In later years when times and things were different and chickens were too expensive to serve with prodigality and children were seen, heard, and obeyed and became the principal topic of conversation when company came, we used to joke to our mother about the good old days of preachers, yellow legged chickens, and seen but not heard children. Bless us how times and conditions have changed.

In later years when my own family and home had been established it was our good fortune to have the pleasure of having a few of those very same preachers, aged though they were, as guests at our table and I have always taken a bit of fiendish delight in twitting them in a casual way about the experiences of our youth and their love of yellow legged chickens.

Since youthful days I have developed a profound respect for the gentlemen of the cloth both Protestant and Catholic for they are honestly endeavoring to do a good work even if they do love the "flesh pots of Egypt" and yellow legged chickens. "To him that hath shall be given and to him that hath not shall be taken away, even that which he hath." Thus endeth another lesson in ancient history.

Seven: Stories and Recollections

HEARTS OF THE HILLS. This tale has nothing to do with local history but serves to show that the human heart will always beat responsive to those in distress no matter where they live.

It was a few minutes before five o'clock on the morning of April 18, 1906, that I had returned from a trip by team to the town of Milton, Calaveras County. At that time I was surgeon for the Union Copper Mining Co. of Copperopolis and was preparing to go to bed for a couple hours' sleep before taking up the usual round of work for the day.

At a few minutes after five there was a rumble as of thunder, which was followed by a series of shocks that seemed to rock the very foundations of the earth beneath us, windows rattled, dishes clattered and in some cases came crashing to the floor, many clocks stopped, furniture skidded about the house, and the old-fashioned drop cord electric lights swayed violently, then all was still; it was an earthquake.

At eight o'clock that morning the local telegraph office opened and a few minutes later the operator came out looking a bit shaken. He called to all who were in the street at that time to come and hear the news. He read a message going over the wire that an earthquake had destroyed San Francisco and that fire was sweeping through the ruins, that thousands had been killed, that other thousands were fleeing the ruins or congregating in the parks, that a tidal wave had swept the Cliff House into the sea, along with a lot of other wild rumors. Of course we of that mountain mining town were horrified for many had relatives and friends living in the stricken city and of course feared the worst. Then came the governor's call for cooked food to be sent to the survivors. A local committee was formed, the barbed wire telephone got busy, and every farm and ranchhouse within reach was contacted for miles around, mounted messengers were sent to those who had no telephone; all were told the news and the needs and to bake bread, hard boil eggs, and boil hams and bring their contributions into town early. Sacks of flour, cases of eggs, and hams were purchased at the local stores by those who had no homes and these things were sent to homes where they could be prepared for shipment.

The whole community got busy, fires burned all night in every home in all that section, even after ovens full of fine homemade bread were turned out, hundreds of dozens of good fresh ranch eggs were hard boiled along with some fifty hams and by eight o'clock the next morning all the food had been collected and packed in cases, labeled, and loaded in two big freight wagons, the loads were not so heavy as they were bulky.

People for miles around had come into town to offer help, hear all the news, and see the loads off to the rail head at Milton, fifteen miles away. As the two teams started on their way, a mighty cheer rose from the people massed in the one main street of the little mining town, someone started singing "America" and all joined in—ranchers, miners, cowpunchers, men, women, and children. Many eyes were filled with tears, some wept audibly, the moment was tense and full of happiness for our community had answered the governor's call for help, and like true Americans the people had responded with all they had.

After the teams had disappeared around a bend in the road the crowd still stood spellbound in the street, when someone mentioned the fact that all the ham, eggs, and flour in town had been sent away and that it might be many days before other supplies could be freighted in. For a minute the assemblage seemed dazed as though wondering what next to do, when one old grizzled and bearded miner stepped forward, hat in hand into the circle, tears streaming down his weather-beaten cheeks, tobacco juice staining his gray beard, and said with as much reverence as if offering a prayer to the Most High, "Folks, I'll tell you what, if we run out of grub, by God we can eat 'jump highs.' " "Jump highs" was a common name for jack rabbits, which were plentiful in all the foothill country.

THE LONG AGO. Looking back through a period of some sixty-odd years, one cannot help to compare the conditions of today with those of long ago. When a small boy, the average family in rural Sonoma County lived more or less alike, and enjoyed themselves as only pioneers knew how.

They were almost self-sufficient, and had to buy but very little from stores, except what you might call raw material, such as farm machinery or material to make the same, and goods to make clothing for nearly all members of the family, except the adult males, and they all wore store clothes, with perhaps a tailor made suit of black broadcloth for dress occasions and Sundays.

My father and mother worked from sunrise to sunset, and they were happy and enjoyed life, their growing family, and the friendship and cooperation of their neighbors. Father ranched, taught school, and figuratively speaking, brought home the bacon. Mother, in addition to doing all her house work, except when my sisters were babies, made all the clothing for herself and us three children, including red flannel underwear, knit stockings, mittens, and mufflers from wool yarn, so that we might be kept warm in winter.

They had no labor-saving gadgets, made butter with an earthen churn and wooden butter bowl and molds, baked bread, did laundry, made soap, roasted coffee beans, and ground sufficient each morning for the breakfast coffee and had time to do fancy work, make wax flowers, paint, study music, besides occasional visits to and from neighbors.

William Shipley and his sister Nell as children. (Courtesy Shipley family.)

Quilting bees were social events, and were thoroughly enjoyed by the ladies of the neighborhood. In the evenings after the day's work was done, especially in winter, the family would gather by the fire in the living room, and after singing a few songs in which all joined, or tried to, mother would sew, knit, or crochet, and father would read aloud from some of the masters, or history, sometimes poetry, or the Youths Companion, and we were all happy and contented. We needed little outside entertainment or diversion.

I can remember the old candle molds, and how they were used to make candles from mutton tallow. In those days when one neighbor would kill an animal, he would divide with the neighbors, and in this way the supply of fresh meat for all was maintained. I can also remember going with father to the mill over on Sulphur Creek to have corn ground into meal, and for pay the miller would take his toll, a certain portion of the meal.

There was also a smoke house, and every fall salt pork, hams, and bacon were prepared and hung on pegs in the ceiling beams of the cellar, along with rows of winter apples and pears on straw-covered shelves, for the winter season.

They used to dry and preserve their own fruit, so outside of buying flour, sugar, salt, green coffee berries, tea, molasses, and material for clothes and a few store clothes for father, the ranch produced nearly everything we needed. We were able to maintain ourselves, save a little, and were supremely happy. As we grew up, each child was assigned a definite chore to do, not only for the help it gave our parents, but it taught responsibility.

Today we are kept busy taking care of labor-saving devices, running pell-mell about the country, sticking our noses into other people's business, and do not get half the enjoyment out of our life our forebears did; in the words of the Good Book, "Vanity, vanity, all is vanity."

HOW GEORGE WILCOX KILLED THE BEAR.

The George Wilcox ranch was out beyond what is now the Samuels ranch. The Bishop ranch and the Wickerham [sic— correct spelling is Wickersham] ranch with the Flat Ridge ranch were all neighbors in those days. It was the Wickerhams who were murdered by a Chinese cook back in the '80s. Old Tennessee Bishop was one of the early sheriffs of Sonoma County.

Old George Wilcox, who used to get his mail and do his trading in Healdsburg, was one of those hardy pioneers who helped to develop the northern portion of Sonoma County; at the time of this story he owned a couple thousand acres of that wild and rugged section surrounding Mt. Tom, which rears its gigantic mass above the surrounding hills and dales. Most of the country was not fenced and the stock used to roam the hills.

Bears as well as other predatory animals were quite numerous, necessitating the corraling of the young calves at night. These corrals were made of oak posts set on end about seven or eight feet high, and very close together, with wing fences composed of saplings and wire in which to drive the cattle.

One day old George was out repairing one of these wing fences, using a heavy hatchet which was easier carried than an axe, to cut the necessary poles and drive them in place.

He had laid his gun, together with his coat, under a sapling some distance away, and had been working industriously for perhaps half an hour, and just finished cutting a white oak sapling about as thick as a man's arm and four or five feet long, when he happened to glance behind him and spied a big, brown bear intently watching his operations. George was a man of quick temper and bears he despised above all animals, as they frequently killed and ate his young calves and colts.

At the sight of this bear, so close at hand, and so interested in his work, he naturally flew into an unusual rage, and gave the bear the cussing of its life, winding up his verbal castigation by hurling the hatchet at the bruin.

This was a fatal mistake. It hit the bear a nasty wallop and riled its otherwise apparently peaceful disposition. The bear growled and charged. To run for his gun would be out of the question, as the bear happened to be between him and the sapling where reposed that trusty weapon. George knew it was a case of fight and not run, so he picked up the white oak sapling and when the bear came close enough to be within good range he brought it down with a resounding whack alongside the bear's head, which evidently caused the bear to see a series of comets, shooting stars, and other celestial objects, for he fell to the ground with a dull thud, but like a pugilist that has been knocked down, he arose and returned to the battle madder than a wet hen.

Old George stood his ground, and as the bear rushed the second time, landed another powerful wallop with the stout white oak sapling across the head. It became a case of up and down with the bear. Every time he rose to the attack, old George would bean him, with the result that he would go down and out, but only for a moment. Before George could land him again he would regain his fighting attitude and charge, only to receive another wallop.

One blow from George's club would have killed an ox, for he was a powerful man and was wielding the club for every ounce of strength he possessed, for the bear sure meant business. As the bear's skull was thick, its skin loose, and its fur soft and fluffy, the blows merely served to stun it. However, after some fifteen or twenty minutes of fierce scrapping, old George landed one crushing blow behind the ear which laid the bear cold. George drew his knife and cut his throat before he had a chance to regain consciousness and renew the attack.

After that old George never unbuckled his gun while fixing fence or doing any other work while upon the range. He had been taught a lesson that came near costing his life.

I went to school in Healdsburg with some of George Wilcox's younger brothers and sisters.

A CAMPING TRIP. It was one summer vacation in the late '80s; Will Bell, Julius Fried, Lydon Shaw, and myself made up a camping trip all by ourselves, to go over to the coast via Guerneville, Stewarts Point, and Skaggs Springs.

Will Bell and Lydon Shaw furnished the horses and harness. Julius and I rented for a small sum an old spring wagon which was not in use, from A. Bonton. It was rather a rickety old wagon, and we had to soak up the felloes to keep the tires from rattling, but it served our purpose.

We loaded our grub, bedding, extra old clothes, fishing tackle, hay and grain for the horses, and an old muzzle loading shotgun into the rig, and early one morning set out on our great adventure. As we left town a large black dog insisted on following, and as we did not know who belonged to the dog, and could not make him go back, we finally accepted him as a member of the party.

The first night we camped on Austin Creek, a few miles from Cazadero, and after fixing camp we fished in the stream for about an hour, each caught a fine mess of trout; we were all delighted and feasted that night, and the next morning on fried trout, fried potatoes, onions, and bacon, with bread and coffee—food fit for the gods of Olympus.

Next day we reached Stewarts Point, after having stopped to see Fort Ross en route. As the roads were steep and the load heavy, three would walk up hill, even sometimes helping push the wagon, but we all rode down hill and on the level, and as there was little level road we did a heap of walking, and had to repair the brake shoes on the wagon every night.

At Stewarts Point we stayed in an old barn as a rain squall greeted us for two days. We caught no fish and as soon as the sun came out we packed up and started for Gualala River via Skaggs Springs Road. We found a good campsite that evening by the stream; fishing was good and we had a great time, eating and fishing and we all ate a lot.

One night as we were rolled up in our blankets by the campfire, one of the boys gave a blood-curdling shriek and boiled out of his blankets in terror. It seemed the dog had come over and licked his face, waking him, and in the dim light of the fire he thought it was a grizzly bear. Of course the commotion roused the rest in highly excited state, but order and quiet was again restored when we found it was only the dog.

Due to our marvelous appetites, by the sixth day out our food was getting low and we had to start home the morning of the seventh day, with only onions and coffee for breakfast, as all other supplies were eaten and were we hungry. We were nearly famished. When we reached Cozzens Store in the upper Dry Creek Valley, we had enough small change among us to buy two cans of corn beef and a box of soda crackers, and how we did fill up, food never tasted so good before. That afternoon we reached home, happy, hungry, and dirty, but we had a marvelous time.

A SWARM OF BEES. Seeing an article in a late issue of the *Tribune*, relating an experience of W. A. Tillinghast with bees in his sweater, reminded me of an experience with a swarm of bees in the summer of 1886, while working for J.H. Curtiss, whose ranch was on the river below the county bridge.

It was one of those warm days late in June, and the crew consisted of the Curtiss boys, one or two Passalacqua boys, and myself were pitting, sulphering, and spreading early plums to dry.

In those days there were few prunes being raised, and dried plums were in demand. My job was to operate an old-style hand-and-foot power pitter; the juice would squirt as the pit was forced out of the plum, and we were covered from head to foot. As the weather was hot we wore few clothes—a hat, a hickory shirt, a pair of blue or brown jeans overalls, with socks and shoes. Some even went barefoot.

While thus busily engaged in an effort to feed the nation dried plums, we noticed a swarm of bees buzzing about in the air over our heads, and before long they began to light on my head and shoulders. Evidently the queen bee had mistaken my old brown juice-soaked hat for a hive and lit under the edge of the brim; in a few seconds several thousand bees had made my hat their home. They crowded all over my face, neck, and shoulders, humming a song of perfect contentment—they even crawled down inside my shirt, producing a rather unpleasant sensation, as well as being a bit critical.

To have fought them off would have been the height of folly, for if not frightened or disturbed, they would not sting. The rest of the gang kept a respectful distance, as I slowly walked across the road to the river where there was a swimming hole several feet deep.

Carefully removing my shoes and socks, pants, and finally the shirt, by dropping it down and stepping out, clad only in an old hat and a swarm of happy bees, which seemed to be having the time of their lives, I waded out into the water until it came up to my armpits, and then ducked under and moved upstream a few feet. Coming to the surface, my swarm of uninvited and unwanted bees were spread out on the water and moving rapidly downstream. Wet bees are harmless, the old hat was rescued, clothes donned, the day saved, and work at the plum pitter resumes.

Casualties—one swarm of bees—no great loss, for there is an old saying among the pioneers as to the value of bees, that "A swarm in May is worth a ton of hay," "A swarm in June is worth a silver spoon," and "A swarm in July is not worth a fly."

HORSES AND HORSEMEN. In the '70s, '80s, and '90s many Healdsburgers were horse conscious as the noble equine was in those days the principal means of transportation for both business and pleasure, and we had some mighty fine horses.

Harvey Peck, J.M. Bailhache, the Van Allen brothers, Wolf Rosenberg, T.S. Merchant, and others owned, drove, and admired fine high stepping buggy horses. In those days nearly everybody who had to go places had some kind of rig, some gorgeous, some others just plain but useful and still others more or less like the last rose of summer.

Some owned and rode fine saddle horses and how they loved to show off their mounts or driving horses. Of course no one could accuse them of personal pride, it was their horse and rigs they gloried in displaying. Byrd Brumfield was a superb horseman, and boasted that he could ride anything with hair on or had four hoofs.

It so happened there was a man in Petaluma had a very fine saddle horse, a beautiful blue roan who would occasionally light in and buck him off, so he invited Byrd to ride him and take out the kinks. This horse was noted for speed and wind. No road was too long, so Byrd concluded to give him a real workout; at sun-up one spring morning, Byrd mounted this spirited horse and set out for Boonville, which was a little over one hundred miles by the crooked roads of that day.

Town after town was passed, on through Cloverdale and out Boonville Road at a stiff gait with only occasional stops to water the horse and for the rider to refresh himself.

Roland Truitt, age eighty-six, was grand marshal in the 1927 July Fourth Parade. (Courtesy Robert Hassett, Healdsburg Museum collection.)

Late in the afternoon the horse and rider, leather creaking, hoofs pounding, entered the long main street of Boonville. Byrd plied the rowels to give the horse added fire so as to make a grand entry into that sleepy mountain town and wake up the inhabitants who might happen to be about the streets.

The horse was covered with foam, the rider and mount a bit jaded from the long ride, but when Byrd pulled rein in front of the old Boonville Hotel, then owned by a couple by the name of Berry, the horse stuck his nose between his front feet, arched his back and did some fancy old-fashioned worm fence bucking. His front end was high in the air one second and his hind quarters the next.

Byrd was surprised, taken off guard, and in a short time described a parabola and left in the soft dirt of the street.

(This story was told to me by the late John F. Mulgrew.)

HOW ALBERT POPPED THE QUESTION. Albert Dingle was seated by the big log fire in old Si Lawrence's living room; at the opposite side of the hearth, all resplendent in her best bib and tucker, sat pretty Polly, old Si's youngest and only remaining daughter. Albert was sparking Polly and had been doing so every night since last October. It was now almost spring—in fact, the March storm was at its height and without the wind howled and the rain beat in sympathy with the desolation in his soul.

Albert was a young man of few words but an ardent lover. He would sit by the fire at a safe distance from the lady of his desire, and gaze in rapture at her, with but an occasional comment on his, or a timid yes or no in answer to a question on the part of the fair one, with long and oppressive silences between. He was what you might call an habitual lover for he had sparked a new girl in the same quiet manner every winter for the past ten years, and had become the joke in the neighborhood—some folks went so far as to assert that if he did not succeed in catching Polly he would be doomed to be an old bachelor, for he had worn out his welcome with all the other girls in the Dry Creek Valley by his long continued silent wooing.

On this particular evening Albert had been even more silent and thoughtful than ever, for he was revolving the momentous question in his mind how he could screw up his courage to break the glad tidings of great joy to Polly of his love and ask her to be his wife. His courage was rising and falling like the waves of the sea, at one time the words trembled on his lips only to sink again into the bottomless pit of despair as a wave of timidity would overwhelm him.

It was now past midnight and Albert picked up his old green umbrella from beside the mantel piece to prepare for his departure. He never left before midnight unless requested, it had been his custom through all these years of silent courtship.

Awkwardly poising the umbrella in Polly's direction, his face set and pale, his feet fidgeting nervously as a wave of heroic effort welled up in his being, he made a thrust at Polly as though he would stab her in the heart with the metal tip of the old umbrella and at the same time saying in a hoarse whisper, through the great lump in his throat that he was trying to swallow, "Polly, I'd like to poke you."

"Why, Albert! why would you like to poke me?" said Polly, blushing and almost overcome by this sudden flow of speech. "Cause you won't marry me," cried Albert in a firmer tone, his courage now rising higher. "You'd never asked me," cooed Polly, greatly relieved. "Well, I asks you now," said Albert, almost shouting with joy, and the agony was over. They were married the following June, and lived happily together for over forty years.

NO HAWG. The following story was told by my maternal grandmother, Mrs. C.E. Dutcher, and it must be true, for she was a devout Methodist and a firm believer in the Ten Commandments. It happened shortly after coming to Healdsburg in 1870, before the days of modern thought, carefully balanced diets, slenderizing, labor-saving gadgets, and the New Deal.

The Dutcher family owned and operated a ranch known as the Dr. Cook place, fronting on the road down the river from the county bridge, only in those days there was no bridge, just a ford in the summer and a ferry in the winter. They had one farmhand called John who took his meals with the family, as was the custom in those primitive days. It was also the custom to feed the men their breakfast first so they could get out to work early as in those golden days everyone worked from before sunup to long after dark, especially the ranchers. This particular farmhand was a big man with a prodigious appetite and an almost superhuman capacity for food.

Grandmother Dutcher was a good cook and was justly celebrated for her sourdough buckwheat hotcakes, and when all smeared with fresh butter and smothered in syrup, they were good enough to make a sick angel rouse from its lethargy, sit up, and bat its eyes. As a small boy I have eaten ten or twelve for breakfast myself without getting cramp colic.

After eating a goodly breakfast of ham or bacon, fried eggs, fried potatoes, and other things including air tights, they usually topped off with a flock of hotcakes and coffee, just as a bracer for the day's labor. These hotcakes were not typical western variety half an inch thick, big as a dinner plate, and six to the stack, but were more ladylike as to thickness, diameter, and texture, being light as a feather.

On this morning John had eaten his usual large breakfast and had piled away several stacks of hotcakes and as the cakes happened to be especially good that morning, he asked for more, so grandmother proceeded to bake griddle after griddle full (five cakes to the griddle) which were eaten with relish until John finally pushed back from the table smacking his lips with one uneaten cake on his plate. Having eaten ninety-nine cakes, grandmother suggested that he eat the last cake and make it an even hundred to which he replied in some disgust "Do you think I would make a hawg of myself for one hotcake."

THE BLIND TUCKERS. It must have been in the early '70s that Mr. and Mrs. John Tucker (the blind Tuckers, as everyone referred to them when speaking of them) came to Healdsburg and opened the first notion and candy store on a cash and carry basis, which was located on Powell Street, about the middle of the block between West and Center Streets.

Being totally blind and not needing a great deal of space, they occupied rooms in the rear of their store, all of which was kept immaculately clean. They had a fairly good stock of merchandise for those days, including toys, dolls, stationery, some books, stick and broken candies, nuts, and even had an old-fashioned peanut roaster. Even though they could not see, they knew where everything on their shelves, under the counter, or in the show cases was located, as well as its price.

They kept no books, paid cash for their goods, and sold for cash. They were able to distinguish their customers and call them by name as soon as they entered the store just by the sound of their voices after a few visits. They knew money by its feel, could distinguish the different gold and silver pieces, knew the copper coins of 1¢, 2¢, and 3¢ denominations and the 5¢ and 25¢ silver pieces, a few of which were still in circulation. Paper money was beyond them, but as there was very little in circulation, this was a minor trouble but they did know good money from bad just by its feel.

Among other candies carried in their showcase were large slabs of pink, yellow, and white taffy which had to be broken with a little hatchet. Both Tuckers were expert in breaking up candy by this means, could set the scales and weigh out the exact amount desired, never cheating themselves or the customer. They were honest as the days were long and expected the same treatment from others but their wits (were) keen and sometimes (they) had to refuse bad money that some party with evil intent tried to palm off on them.

On one occasion a customer asked for a certain kind of notebook. John was having trouble locating it, when his good wife, who was present, stepped behind the counter, picked it up from the shelf saying, "Here it is, John, I can see better than you can."

Besides doing all her own housework and helping in the store, Mrs. Tucker did knitting and hand sewing, enjoyed callers so as to get all the news of the day, for she was interested in all that went on about her.

How they lost their sight no one seemed to know, for at that time in our history most people never asked pertinent or embarrassing questions, still believing in the old-time western doctrine of letting every man kill his own snakes, it was not good form to be unduly inquisitive. They both wore dark glasses so as to hide their eyes from view and with all this handicap they were happy and successful, accumulating a snug competence.

Sunday afternoons when weather permitted they would take long walks together, John directing the way by means of a buggy whip with which he felt his way along sidewalks, across streets and, when out of the business district, by the fences.

Mrs. Tucker was short and a bit fat, would kink her right arm into his left for guidance and in this way they would enjoy the sunshine together. John would go about the business section with as much precision as if he had perfect eyesight.

Along about 1890 they sold out and retired; they have both been gone these many years but no doubt the old-timers will recall them with a feeling of pleasure, for they liked everybody and everybody liked them.

A UNIQUE PROPOSAL. My mother used to tell the following story, long long ago, so it must be true. It all happened way back in the days when maids were shy and some of the young men were green as grass, not long after she arrived in Healdsburg in the spring of 1870.

Like nearly all young men since Cain made sheep's eyes at the girls over in the land of Nod, the pioneer boys in Healdsburg admired the pretty girls, although some were too bashful or afraid to pop the question. It so happened, as at present, there were many very fine looking girls of marriageable age in and about the old hometown, who loved to be admired and would not be averse to accepting the right young man should he come a-courting.

In the case of Jim, the young man of this story, he was an only son of a fairly well-to-do farmer and had good prospects, but he was timid and afraid when it came to the girls. His paw and maw were very anxious that he should wed the charming daughter of an equally prosperous neighbor, so that by combining the two families and farms a great dynasty might be founded of which both families could be proud. So the young man's father one day told him that he was now old enough to have a wife, and that he would do well to shine up to Mollie, the daughter of their neighbor, for she had all the qualifications of a good wife from every point of view. She was good looking, a good cook and housekeeper, would make a good mother, and would some day inherit quite a bit of worldly goods and land.

The young man admitted that he had for a long time secretly admired Mollie very much and had thought the same thing but did not know how to go about it, or what to say. The wise father advised his son as follows—"Now, Jim, some fine evening you clean up, put on your best go-to-meeting clothes and go over to Mollie's house. You knock on the door and no doubt she will open it to greet you. Then you can say—good evening, Miss Mollie, a fine evening, many stars in the firmament. She will likely invite you in, one thing will lead to another and then you can ask her for her company."

As fate would have it, Jim selected a beastly stormy night to make his first call on pretty Mollie, and all dolled up his very best, with fear and trembling he knocked on the front door of her home. As was expected, Mollie opened the door to greet him with her most alluring smile when again a sad fate intervened, for Jim got all flustered, you might say had a spell of the jitters. He forgot his father's instructions and words of wisdom as to how to approach the lady of his dreams, and blurted out: "Evening Miss, fine evening, many stars in the fumblement, you'll invite me in, one thing will lead to another and after a while I'll ask for your trumpery."

Needless to say, Jim's noble effort bogged down right there. He was seized with panic and beat it for home. Later that season Mollie wedded another man, and Jim was treed and captured by a young widow who did most of the courting and all lived in blissful ignorance ever after. The great family dynasty the old folks had set their hearts on failed to materialize, and thus endeth another lesson in ancient history.

A GRAND OLD INDIAN. Captain Jack started his long journey into the happy hunting ground about twenty-five years ago in his little cabin on the poverty-stricken land generously given to the Indians by the politicians of the Government Indian Service, a few miles east of Hopland. At the time of his passing he was very old, totally blind, and almost helpless, with his good wife of many, very many moons, numerous relatives, and tribal members present to chant him, Indian fashion, on his way and mourn the passing of a fallen chief.

As a boy he had with his tribe roamed the hills and valleys of the Russian River country from Ukiah to the river's mouth and had been schooled in all the lore and craft of the Pomo Indians, of which he was a sub-chief, until the death of his brother-in-law some years before when he inherited the chieftainship.

The dignity and responsibility of his position was to him a serious matter; his sense of honor was one of the highest, his word was as good as a bond or better, he was honest, just above reproach, and his manners were superior to many of his pale face brothers.

In his youth he had gone shy an eye by accident and always wore a black leather patch held in place by a buck skin thong to cover the defect; otherwise he was a very fine looking old brave.

Manuel Cordova (far right) and Alfred Elgin (second from right) give Pomo dance tips to Julius Myron Alexander, c. 1920s.

Some thirty years ago there was a great demand for Indian baskets and other ornamental trinkets and as I bought many of their art works through the Captain as an intermediary with his people, for myself and others, we became friends. For small favors in his behalf he gave me several beautiful baskets, a feather ceremonial head piece, a string of wampum containing six hundred shell beads, a bow and deer skin quiver with four arrows made by himself and his squaw, to whom he always referred as an Indian queen, together with several other Indian relics. (The Shipley collection is (was) on display in the Sonoma County Historical Society Museum at 557 Summerfield Road, Santa Rosa, open Sundays.)

At times he would be quite talkative and tell of his early life and the customs of his people before the white men came to spoil life for the primitive red man, yet he held no grudge against the stronger race. In speaking of laws and customs, once he compared the simple direct Indian tribal law to our complicated and at times irrational legal system and rather queer customs.

He said, "Our people had a few laws but they were good and just; if a member of the tribe broke a law, we told him to go; if he did not go we kill him." Banishment meant that the one exiled had to leave naked without arms or any equipment, even his family had to be left behind; he had to face the elements bare-handed and what was worse no other tribe would receive the law breaker, so death was more often chosen than banishment.

125

Another custom which to our minds might seem cruel was when a member of the tribe became too old to hunt or follow the tribe in its seasonal migrations and was helpless, one of the braves near of kin was delegated to approach the aged one from the rear and crush his skull in with a war club, thus putting him or her out of misery.

The young Indians were taught to venerate their parents, relatives and elders, obey their chiefs and tribal customs. As to religion the Pomo Indians were sun or fire worshippers, believing in the Great Spirit, typified by the glorious effulgence of the rising sun, the giver of light, heat, and all things good for his children, the Indians.

They also believed in signs and omens both good and bad and in evil spirits that moved about in the darkness and like all other Indian tribes from coast to coast the hereafter was a Happy Hunting Ground, where spring was eternal, with game of all kinds plentiful, and no inter-tribal wars or other misunderstandings to mar their everlasting happiness.

While the old Captain had partially espoused the Catholic faith, he firmly believed in the teachings and traditions of his ancestors, and who can say but that the laws, customs, and religion of these simple untutored savages were not as good and as beautiful as those we whites respect and love?

As a mark of friendship and confidence the old Captain made me his blood brother and a member of the tribe, and while this gesture on his part may not be rated very high by some moderns, to that simple honest old Indian it came from his heart and was the greatest gift within his power to bestow. To me, pale face, it meant as much as if conferred by king, prince, potentate, or an established government.

May the grass be ever green and the game plenty in the Happy Hunting Ground for old Captain Jack, a grand old Indian. (An etching of Captain Jack is on the cover of the book *Wild Oats in Eden.*)

THE KINDNESS OF GENERAL VALLEJO. It was the custom of most parents, when we were children, to tell their offspring stories of adventures that befell them and their ancestors, because books, papers, and magazines were few and hard to get.

In this way traditional history had been handed down from father to son since the beginning of time and is an art that has almost been lost in this modern time. Grandparents, especially grandmothers, delighted in telling ghost stories which both thrilled and frightened the youngsters.

My father and mother used to tell us three children stories of their early life and of historic events which, to me now wandering down the sunny hillside of life, are cherished memories never to be forgotten. The following story was told to me by father when I was a small boy, so it must be true. My grandfather, R.J. Shipley, came to California via the Horn in 1850 and two years later sent for his wife and my father, who was then a boy of nine. They arrived via the Isthmus of Panama in the fall of 1852 and rented farming land on shares near Sonoma. In addition to caring for the farm, Grandfather Shipley conducted a small meat business, i.e., he would kill one or two fat steers a week, doing the butchering late at night and making deliveries early the next morning, as there was no means of refrigeration during the summer months. In winter it was different, as meat would keep for several days.

This was back in the days when General Vallejo was in his prime and quite an outstanding figure in the booming young town. My father would go on the spring wagon to hold the horses while his father made deliveries of meat in front of a store in the business section. Father, then a boy of about ten, was holding the team while his immediate ancestor was in the store purchasing supplies.

A stray chicken wandered by and a dog took after it as dogs will do. As the squawking, wing-flapping hen with the yapping dog in close pursuit passed in front of the team the latter took fright, bolted, and headed full speed for home south of town. Roads in those days were none too good, so father was bounced out of the seat into the bed of the wagon, still clinging to the reins. Of course he received a vigorous jolting as the careening team and wagon negotiated the ruts and hummocks of the primitive road.

Fortunately it happened that General Vallejo was present, mounted on one of his best saddle horses. He saw the runaway, realized the boy's danger and, being a superb horseman, put spurs to his steed, gave chase and overtook the runaway team about half a mile down the road, seized the bridle of the nigh horse, and succeeded in stopping them without damage being done. Of course grandfather borrowed a saddle horse and gave chase, catching up with the outfit a few minutes after the General had stopped the runaway team.

General Vallejo's first remark was, "Shipley, the boy is all right." Thanks and appreciative greetings were exchanged between the General and my grandfather, the General very politely trying to minimize his rather heroic act. The General was always that way, always the fine gentleman, always ready to do a kindness for others even at his own risk.

Some years ago I told this story to Señora Louisa Vallejo Emparan, the last surviving daughter of the grand old General. Her eyes shined like stars, tears welled up in them, a happy smile spread over her lovely face, and with right hand over her heart as she looked up to the heavens, she exclaimed "Just like my father, he was always considerate of others."

A JOKE ON HARRY BROWN. Back in the day, Prof. C.L. Ennis was head of the local school department, consisting of primary and grammar schools all housed in two old wooden buildings erected on a plot of ground where once was located the first cemetery.

Harry Brown, son of Mr. and Mrs. H.K. Brown, was in the last year of upper class, would soon graduate and take his place in the world of affairs. Harry was quite a blood, or may we say dandy; he dressed well, thought himself about right, and was quite some lady killer. He had some good prospects, his parents were good, substantial, respected people, financially sound and influential in the community, all the world was ahead of him, he would go places, be somebody, and so naturally many of the local girls looked at him with longing in their hearts.

Mrs. Brown, his good mother, was an immaculate housekeeper and tried to instill into her son the same ideas of thrift and order in all things. Now it so happened that

Harry was a bit careless at times and would leave his clothes and other belongings kicking around his room on bed, chairs, or floor, instead of heeding his mother's oft repeated admonition that the closet or bureau drawers were the place for his clothes, shoes, and other trinkets when not in use.

Mrs. Brown was a determined lady and had frequently threatened to send the things she had to pick up after he had left for school to his classroom. Well, Harry had heard this threat so often that he had grown indifferent to his mother's frequent scoldings so he concluded she was just trying to scare him and he paid no heed.

Time passed and still the indifference continued, so one fine morning about the end of school Harry had to make a hurried change into his good school clothes and beat it to prevent being late at roll call, so he left all his clothes which were not too clean, sox, shoes, and all on the floor for his mother to pick up.

When Mrs. Brown came in to make up his room she was horrified, shocked beyond expression at the mess so she determined to make an example of her son's indifference to her teaching. To think was to act. She gathered all his duds into a bundle, called the expressman, and sent them to school with a note to Prof. Ennis requesting him to have Harry bring them home and hang them up as she had so often demanded.

The bundle of old clothes and the note to the Prof. did the work. Harry was taken down many pegs, in fact he came from his high horse with a dull thud, blushed a deep red while the whole class laughed and had a lot of fun.

Well, Harry, feeling a bit crestfallen, took the clothes home, hung them up where they belonged, begged his mother's forgiveness, and never again did he leave home without hanging up his clothes. This story goes to show how a determined mother may correct the indifference and negligence of a heedless son.

AUNT KATE BEAR. Another of the old characters who lived in Healdsburg during the '70s and '80s was Aunt Kate Bear, who resided in a little, old two-room shack with front porch and leanto kitchen in the rear, at the corner of East and Mill Streets. If memory serves me right, she was thin, small, bent under the weight of many years and hard work. Her face was a mass of wrinkles, yet her eyes were bright as stars and, as she had no teeth, her rather long nose and pointed chin almost met when her mouth was closed tight, giving her a weird appearance.

She smoked a clay pipe, black with age and long use, dipped snuff, wore old-style square lens "specks" with brass frames when doing closeup work, had a visible mustache and had a few stray hairs on her chin, all of which added quaintness to her ensemble.

When and where she came from no one seemed to know for she was quite an old-timer when my mother came to town in the spring of 1870. From her looks, her habits, her mode of speech and other indications, she must have come from south of the Mason Dixon Line.

She had a brother, Davy Cook, who, with quite a party including herself and husband, started across the plains in '49 for California. Her husband was killed by Indians, so when she finally arrived in Healdsburg she was a poor, lone widow. There seemed to be no record of what happened to her brother, so in the '80s she was all alone and known to everyone as Aunt Kate.

She always dressed in plain black, wore a poke bonnet of the same somber color, set off by a white-frilled ruching, sewed inside the brim that encircled her face. She wore a gingham apron, usually of dark color except on Sundays, when she would don one of spotless white. It was rumored she had a little nest-egg laid away against her extreme old age when she might be helpless, but to keep the wolf from the door she took in washing, did mending, and plain sewing for a few families.

In fancy I can still see this little old lady hanging out the snowy laundry on the line behind her little house, sun-bonnet and all, as she industriously puffed away at her old clay pipe. This was all way back in the days when it was considered a disgrace to accept charity, go to the county hospital, or the poor farm, so Aunt Kate Bear did her share of work to prevent such a sad ending.

True, some of her neighbors, including Mrs. Geo. Haigh, Madam Cavet, and my mother used to send her in tidbits as good will offerings to a grand old lady. Afternoons when through with her work, if skies were blue and the weather pleasant, she would sit on the front porch in an old rocker, sew or mend as she rocked and smoked her beloved pipe. When the weather was unpleasant she would sit by her front window with a good fire to keep her warm and do the same thing day after day as she watched the rest of the world go by.

It may have been that she could neither read nor write as she never was seen with book or paper, but in her spare time did knitting and sewing. She seldom called on her neighbors and few ever called on her, also she seldom went to church. She tended strictly to her own business and was what might be called a female hermit. In '85 or '86 she took to her bed and in a few days left this earthly sphere for her home on high, where "dust and moth do not corrupt nor thieves break in and steal." The humble home was torn down and a more modern house erected in its place which is now beginning to show the ravages of time.

Thus do we each and all play our part in the scheme of life and in due time are gathered to our fathers, for awhile a faint memory abides and then gradually we are forgotten. Aunt Kate Bear did her share and very best while here on earth, was honest, industrious, paid her bills, did not talk about her neighbors, and minded her own business.

No doubt when she came face to face with her Maker, He said, "Well done thou good and faithful servant; enter thou into the joy of thy Lord."

To Mrs. Alice Haigh Dixon, a daughter of Mrs. George Haigh, this writer is indebted for some of the foregoing information.

UNCLE CHARLES AND AUNT ACHSAH. Ever since Cyrus Alexander settled in the beautiful valley bearing his name in 1840, the descendants and relatives of that brave old pioneer have borne an honored reputation in Healdsburg and vicinity.

Charles Alexander, a nephew of Cyrus, settled in the valley in 1850 and shortly after wedded the daughter of another pioneer whose given name was Achsah (pronounced

Aunt Achsah Alexander and her husband, Charles. Charles was the nephew of Cyrus Alexander.

by most folks "Axie") and they reared a family of three daughters and two sons, Julius M. being the youngest.

In 1880 they sold their ranch in the valley and erected a home on a ranch just across the bridge on the Dry Creek-Guerneville road, near where the railroad crosses the highway. Across the road from their home was the brickyard and planing mill of the Hall family.

Henry Alexander, a brother of Charles, with his family came to Healdsburg from Illinois in 1882. He was a well-to-do retired farmer and lived in a big house which they erected on upper Fitch Street near the present location of the high school. They had a family of four sons and two daughters, as follows: Louis, Frank, Lemuel, Edward, Ida and May.

The three older brothers, with J.M. Alexander, for a time conducted a general merchandise store under the firm name of Alexander Bros. & Co. If memory serves me right it was located between that of Sam Meyer and the Cummings Livery Stable on West Street; later it may have been moved into the Gobbi block when that building was completed.

Charles Alexander and his wife were known to everyone in those days as Uncle Charles and Aunt Achsah; they were devout members of the M.E. church north, where they attended every service, winter and summer, rain or shine, hot or cold. Only serious illness would keep them from the house of God. Uncle Charles was one of the deacons, a class leader, and would alternate with I.A. Delano as superintendent of the Sunday school and teachers of the bible class. Aunt Achsah was a faithful worker in the church, the Sunday school, the Band of Hope, the WCTU, and the Christian Endeavor. Her whole life was devoted to her family, her neighbors, her church, and her God. Taken together they were as fine an old couple as ever inhabited the footstool.

As a small boy attending Sunday school and church I used to look to and admire them as upright, kindly, and Godly people. When Uncle Charles would sit in church paying strict heed to the words of the pastor, passing the contribution plate or attending the other services, his snowy looks, as a fringe around the bald spot atop his head, gave the illustration of a halo.

Most of the youngsters looked up to him as a saint from heaven, our respect for him was that profound. The good deeds of this dear old couple were many and they never let their right hands know what their left hands did. They lived up to the golden rule in spirit and in truth.

Along in the late '80s they were both taken quite ill, perhaps it was the flu or grippe, and were confined to bed for a couple of weeks. The lady members of the church, my mother among them, took turns, two at a time, caring for them. This was long before modern medical science, trained nurses, hot water bottles, and other up-to-date gadgets and jimcracks, so they were both in the same bed to simplify the work of the nurses.

Uncle Charles was recovering but very weak, while Aunt Achsah was at the height of her fever. The doctor in attendance ordered hot stove lids for Uncle Charles' feet as they were cold. While the neighbor ladies were out in the kitchen getting stove lids wrapped in flannel and paper to prevent burning, Uncle Charles happened to get his feet over against the fever-heated ones of Aunt Achsah so when the volunteer nurses arrived with the hot lids he told them that they were not needed as Achsah's feet were warm enough to keep him comfortable.

In spite of the ignorance and simplicity of that far off day both recovered and were soon about their usual mode of life, only to be taken later one at a time to that land of eternal joy, the promised land of their hopes and dreams. A humble tribute with due reverence to two of Healdsburg's worthy citizens.

JEST TOBACKER JUICE. Back in the late '70s when men were bold and brave and the ladies proper and shy, there was a bit of a building boom going on in the old hometown. Then as at present we had a flock of male and female regulators who were always trying to take the joy out of life for others. Sometimes they were referred to as sobsisters, psalmsingers, jayhawkers, sandlappers, or joykillers, rather expressive and picturesque names but they tell the whole story in one word.

There were such organizations as the Band of Hope, the Good Templars, the WCTU, and an occasional ranting, raving, rip-snorting temperance lecturer or revivalist who wanted to make the world over just according to his or her own narrowminded ideas. We have them today, only in greater numbers and with more deadly crazy schemes. The reformers of those days were babes and sucklings.

The following story was told by my great uncle, S.B. Wood, a carpenter who lived with his parents, Mr. and Mrs. James Wood, in a home on Tucker Street not far from where Bro. Adams of the *Tribune* now resides. The story must be true for Uncle Sen, as we all called him, would chuckle with glee, congratulating himself that it happened to his partner instead of himself, for only a few minutes before, he had committed the same awful crime. Then, too, Uncle Sen was honest and could not tell a falsehood.

It seems that S.B. Wood and another carpenter were building a house for a certain single lady who had some rather definite ideas about everything in the world and tobacco in particular. She was plain of dress, not alluring as to face and form—just one of those dear ladies no man would desire unless he was deaf, dumb, and blind. She also had a very caustic tongue and could use it freely.

She parted her hair in the middle, slicked it down and twisted up the wispy remainder in a small pug at the back of her head. The growing bald spot on top of her dome was about the size of a dollar. She abhorred sin in all its forms including alcohol and tobacco, but especially the chewing of the filthy weed—that was awful. This dear lady was precise, prim, set in her ways, and persnickity. You have all seen the types. Some of them even hate themselves.

In those pre-refrigerator days every house had to have an excavated cellar under it to keep things cool in the long hot summer days, and her home had to be as good as the best, so she had a cellar.

Also this spartan lady spent a good deal of time about the place while construction was going on, for she wanted it built right and absolutely according to her own fancy, much to the annoyance of the carpenters who were good workmen and knew how to build a good house.

Now both these carpenters at that time chewed tobacco as did nearly all the men; it was the style, the mark of a gentleman. They would work and chew from seven in the morning to six in the evening with one hour off for lunch and so as not to waste too much time expectorating tobacco juice, they would refrain from spitting until their mouths could hold no more, then go to the window and unload about a bucketful out upon the ground so as not to soil the newly laid floor, which would have caused the lady great anguish, for she would surely see it. She saw everything and might give them a tongue lashing.

To make an appalling story more appalling, the other carpenter stepped to the open window above the entry into the cellar and heaved about a half-pint of rich brown tobacco juice into the atmosphere without looking where he spat. To multiply their troubles the old girl happened to be coming up from the cellar on one of her rounds of inspection without informing them of her presence.

The flood of tobacco juice took her square on top her bald spot and splattered all through her hair. There was a shriek, a yell, a howl of rage as the lady realized the awfulness of the calamity. She made some very acid remarks about filthy tobacco chewers and the degeneracy of one carpenter in particular who did not look where he expectorated, went out to the faucet by the side of the tank house behind the house and, with a pan and a cake of soap, proceeded to wash and re-wash her hair and scalp to cleanse it of contamination of that disgusting tobacco juice.

Of course the carpenter responsible offered a million apologies and was truly sorry, contrite, and humbled as well as shocked as was the lady. After that he provided himself with a box of sawdust and shavings as a receptacle to spit in, instead of using the wide, wide world through an open window.

No wonder Uncle Sen was mighty glad he was not the unfortunate guilty party.

TEMPEST AND SUNSHINE. It may have been in the summer of 1886 or '87, back in those ox team days when most folks were not afraid or ashamed to work, when most everybody not otherwise employed spent the good old summertime picking fruit, grapes, hops, or working in the dryers or fruit canneries and we had no such problems as migrant labor, sympathetic strikes, or out and out communists.

In those happy days our population was self-respecting, self-sufficient, satisfied with things as they were, loyal to their country, in brief, good honest to God Americans. This particular summer several boys about my age, including myself, put in our vacation time working on the fine fruit ranch of "Pappy Gladden" as most people called Mr. W.N. Gladden.

There were also several families working on the Gladden ranch who camped in the cherry orchard near the drying plant. They were simple honest ignorant people just like all the rest of us and of course because they camped out all summer, worked for a living, paid their bills, and minded their own business, no one seemed to look down on them, so they were treated with respect and consideration.

In those far off benighted days nearly everyone had strong backs and weak minds and were willing to do an honest day's work from seven in the morning to six in the evening, for a day's pay which was $1 a day for boys and big girls to a $1.50 to $2 for women and men and everybody was happy as well as fairly prosperous, we had no dreams of old age pensions, social security along with a lot of free this, that, and the other.

Mr. Gladden was more or less like a father to his help, he was willing to show them how he wanted his work done and as most workers took a pride in their work and doing it well he never had to upbraid or fire any of them. One noon time while we were all resting in the shade after lunch, Mr. Gladden was telling his help how on each Christmas morning (his birthday) he would stand on his head, a trick he had been doing ever since he was a small boy; he was at this time about sixty-odd years of age.

Some of the girls present begged him to demonstrate and to their amazement he took a chair, placed his old soft felt hat on the seat for a pad, took hold of the sides to balance himself, and did stand on his head, while the crowd applauded. Incidentally his jack knife and some silver coins fell from his pockets while he was inverted.

The first time I ever saw Mr. Gladden stand on his head in this way was one night when the Methodist choir were having a rehearsal in our home. The old gentleman liked to show how agile he was for a man of his years and took pride in his youthfulness at past sixty.

Now to get to the title of this tale, there was, working for Mr. Gladden at that time, a large family (whose name has been lost in the rubble of the past) consisting of a father, mother, and ten or twelve children, sons and daughters, ranging in age from a babe in arms to a set of twin girls nearly twenty years old. This pair of handsome girls were the same size and form, slender and supple as willow wands, they dressed and looked alike but one was a blonde with violet blue eyes, while the other had curly raven locks with snapping black eyes, and while they were merry, carefree, and happy as the days were long their parents had named them in babyhood Tempest and Sunshine.

It might have been that some freak in the chromosomes caused the difference in color and temperament, otherwise they would have been as alike as two peas in a pod. Tempest, the dark girl, was born a few minutes before her blonde sister Sunshine and the parents, figuring that sunshine always follows a storm, named the girls accordingly, so the girls were appropriately named.

Sometimes they would live up to their picturesque names for the older twin did have a rather peppery temper and could fly off the handle as the old-timers used to say, and make things hum, while the younger twin, whose quiet dignity and self possession was eternal, would come to the rescue and calm her more fiery sister when she kicked over the traces.

The family remained with us only that summer and moved on to greener pastures so they were lost to the community but looking back through the changing panorama of the past they are today as they were then, a puzzle in psychology. Today such girls would be in the movies or some other place of entertainment making their thousands, adulated by the fans, sought after by the play boys, fated and idolized for they had "it" or "Umph," possessed zip, pep, charm, beauty, and that come hither look so alluring to observe, instead of working for $1 a day in the fruit. My! My! How we are evoluting. Thus endeth another lesson in ancient history and a comparison of things as they were and how they are.

TWO OLD BOYS. It was about the middle '80s that my maternal great-grandfather on my mother's mother side lived in upper Tucker Street, neighbor to a family by the name of Blackington. The families of the two old boys were made up of sons, daughters, and in-laws who lived with them.

James Wood, my great-grandfather, was close to eighty, wore a very long snow-white beard, and due to his age was set in his ways. Blackington was about the same age, had long white whiskers, and, due to the same cause, was the possessor of some firm ideas of right and wrong. Both attended the North Methodist Church, both were exemplary in their habits, but could do a little cussing if occasion and necessity demanded. The families were good friends, and enjoyed each other's respect and confidence.

One day a chicken from the Blackington flock got over into the Woods' garden, and proceeded to scratch up things in a big way. Now great-grandfather Wood was very proud of his garden, and also his chicken yard; when the indignation of his Puritanical ancestors rose to choke him, without saying a word, he brought forth a slingshot, and with a smooth stone popped off the chicken. The old boy had become very expert with a slingshot, for by that means he kept birds out of his fruit trees, garden, and berry patch. To have hid or eaten the offending chicken was unthinkable, so it was heaved over into the Blackington's backyard.

Blackington happened to see the whole act from a back window, so in anger he went out, picked up the dead chicken, and said a few warm words to his neighbor, James Wood, which were returned in full measure, and the feud was on.

They took to upbraiding one another whenever they came within hailing distance, and would toss clods of dirt at each other over the picket fence separating their properties. On the Woods' side of this fence there was a row of thrifty blackberry vines, and the old boys would, when not watched by their respective relations, skulk along this fence in an endeavor to clout one another with a clod or a club.

One day when none of the younger members of the family were about the old boys happened to pop up just opposite each other, and each reached out and grabbed the other's patriarchal beard, and the fight was on. They pulled whiskers, cuffed each other a bit, but most of the battle was verbal. It did not last long for the hubbub soon brought the respective families to the rescue and the old boys were separated. Casualties consisted of a few chin whiskers pulled out, a few minor scratches, and badly hurt feelings. Then the Methodist preacher was called in, and the old boys were shown the error of their ways, became repentant, forgave each other, shook hands, and were good friends again for quite some time.

THE TOWN SOT. It was in those carefree days when large schooners of beer sold for 5¢, hard liquor was only 10¢, and the drinker could help himself to a one-, two-, or three-finger shot of "nose paint" without question, as his fancy pleased, that Healdsburg had a few outstanding or rather notorious drunkards, there may even be a few today, who knows.

Of all the dipsomaniacs when I was a small boy, the most outstanding was an old man known by several aliases, such as "Whiskey Jack," "Old Jack," and several others expressive of his appearance and condition.

His name was John Mills; where he came from no one seemed to know and there is no record of his passing on into Glory, but he did hang about Healdsburg for a good many years. He was old and grizzled, with a bald spot on his rather sparsely covered dome of thought. He was scabby, with red watery eyes, the lower lids of which hung away from the eyeballs, giving him a rather repulsive look. His nose had a gorgeous whiskey blossom, being almost purple, and his skin was like parchment as a result of age plus the long continued use of ardent spirits and of dirt.

He would tremble as with palsy until he had absorbed several ounces of whiskey when he would become as steady as a sod house. As soon as the alcohol had steadied his shaken nerves his eyes would be a clear blue and in their depths lurked a gleam of light or fire that showed he had seen and known better days and was possessed of a fine education. He did no work, yet always got by with few wants. He wore other people's castoff clothing and slept in an old shack back of one of the hotels. Life to him was just one drink of whiskey after another.

Whiskey was all that he lived for. He worshipped it as a heathen would worship an idol. Of course each morning before breakfast all drinks were free in those days in the local bars, so Jack would rouse himself from his alcoholic lethargy, make the rounds of

Shipley and friends probably learned at least some of their childhood wisdom from Frank Madeira, a.k.a. Sam the Cheerful Liar, who wrote articles for the Healdsburg Tribune. *Here he demonstrates how to use shoe leather for advertising purposes.*

the saloons, imbibing one large shot of snake juice at each of the six or seven bars located about the plaza. Then he would be steadied and ready for breakfast from one of the garbage cans behind the hotels, unless he found someone who would buy him a few more drinks; he would rather drink than eat.

He harmed no one but himself, was never combative, always polite, for at some time in his life he had been an educated gentleman and could no doubt hold his head up with the best of the human race. He could recite Shakespeare by the mile and when it came to mathematics he was a wizard. No column of figures was too large for him to add, no two numbers too great for him to subtract, and he could multiply and divide, cube and square numbers and extract the square or cube roots in his head. He was a natural-born lightning calculator and was always correct.

For a drink or two he would gladly show off those marvelous gifts and no matter how far gone he was in drink, his mind would carry on. He never spoke of his past so to all who saw him daily he was an enigma. His whole time and attention being devoted to the acquiring of alcohol and more alcohol. His favorite expression was "Say, friend, please give poor old Jack a drink."

Every town in the wild and wooly west has had its unusual, odd, picturesque, or outstanding characters, both good and bad. Old Jack was one such and while he toiled not, neither did he spin nor gather into barns, yet his Heavenly Father fed him with husks the swine did eat—from the swill barrels behind the hotels.

A BABY CASE AND A DOG. It was in the month of February, perhaps 1910, that shortly after breakfast one morning a telephone call came to attend a maternity case at a ranch house two miles east of the Geysers and at an elevation of at least 2,000 feet above that celebrated resort and landmark.

The winter had been severe and as a result the eighteen miles of mountain road from Cloverdale to the Geysers was washed out in many places, in others filled with slides, some bridges and culverts were gone. Fallen trees and other debris obstructed the road. To make the trip by team was out of the question, so saddle horses had to be taken as the only means of transportation. To make the trip alone would be hazardous for a mis-step by a horse or a caving bank might mean instant catastrophe. A man who was a good all-round, outdoor expert from the stable where horses were rented went with me.

Our equipage, i.e., the babycatching outfit, divided into two bundles wrapped in oilskins, was tied behind the cantles of the saddles along with medical and surgical grips and with waterproof slickers to ward off possible rain squalls, we set out on an errand of necessity.

When it came to fording Sulphur Creek a few miles east of town, we had to climb up into the saddles as the water came up over half way on the horses' sides; they were just short of swimming. In places we had to make detours around the heads of the gulches, in others get off and walk to show the horses that it was possible to get through. It was a great trip and it was mid-afternoon before arriving at the old Geysers Hotel, which was destroyed by fire a few years ago.

My companion remained at the Geysers and a man from the mountain with two horses met me on the east bank of the stream to help complete the journey. We had to cross the raging torrent on a foot bridge made of two-by-twelve-foot planks, fastened together by wire end-to-end and supported by two wire cables anchored to trees on either bank. It was a rickety, wobbly affair, but it served the purpose.

Then up the steep winding trail, the last mile of which was under a foot of snow, the ranch house perched in the clouds at that time of year. This house had been built by a young man who had come west from New York for his health; he had taken up the 160 acres on which it stood because it had some fine bench land, plenty of springs, a wonderful view, a world of fine timber with good pasture for animals, and a place to regain his health and establish a home. Every stick of lumber, the hardware, furniture, and other supplies had to be taken up the mountain by pack animals or snaked up on a sled drawn by an ox-team, in places using block and tackle to ease the strain on the animals. He had built a very attractive house in a clearing with all necessary outbuildings and equipment, and, because he was lonely, he looked about for a helpmate and as there were several families with marriageable daughters living in the Sulphur Creek Canyon he did not have to advertise for a wife, but in due time married a daughter of one of his good neighbors.

Among other things his charming wife brought to the home was a big shepherd dog she had raised from a pup. This dog had been her constant companion, had watched over her as carefully as a mother, she was the apple of his dog's eye, he was her guardian and slave day and night, nothing could have harmed her while he had the breath of life, for he was a powerfully big brute, with a heart of gold.

Well, we reached the domicile near the mountain's top just before dark, and after inspecting the patient, the preparations of her mother and a neighbor lady for the reception and pronouncing them satisfactory, a hearty meal was enjoyed by all, and we were ready for any eventuality. When the party began to get lively the dog became agitated, showed so much interest, apparent distress, and became so pesty that the man of the house took him by the collar, and, in spite of his protest, put him out of the house. As soon as the door was shut he began to howl, whine, cry, and bark by turn and scratch on the door. He knew what was going on and wanted to do his share.

He would run round and round and round the house, keeping up a fuss, would look in at the windows and beg to be let in, his distress was pitiful, his knowledge almost human. Shortly after midnight, a baby boy arrived and cried lustily, the dog's fussing changed from that of abject misery to barks and yelps of ecstatic joy. He came to the door and with nose to the threshold sniffed the air, whining softly at the same time, gently pawing at the door. As soon as the baby was fixed up, placed in a padded clothes basket, and the other muss cleared away and all ship-shape, the door was opened and the faithful dog invited into the family circle. He walked softly into the room showing keen interest, went over to the bed where lay the idol of his heart, put his paws on the edge, raised himself up so he could look into her eyes, softly whining, as he gazed at her with all the admiration of his canine soul in his expressive eyes, gently touched her cheek with his nose and as if satisfied got down from the bed, walked over to where the basket was on the floor, took a long look at the sleeping infant, gently nuzzled it once with his tongue, then lay down beside it and went to sleep with one eye open.

He remained there all the rest of the night and would rouse up, take a look when anyone came near, and when satisfied all was well, wag his tail, smile, and resume his sleeping vigil.

During the next few years, it was my pleasure and duty to make other trips to this same home for similar and other reasons but not in such a stormy season as the one in hand, and the dog faithfully watched over each new baby and the others as well. He was with them day and night, never forgetting the young mother, who was his first charge. He would come to her many times a day, lay his head in her lap, look up into her eyes, wag his tail, softly "woof" at her until he received a pat on his head, then go happily back to the care of the three little tots.

When the family sold out and moved to Canada to take advantage of a generous offer of the Canadian government of grants of land, the father, mother, three small children, and the aging dog went as one family.

The dog was almost human, in fact, more to be trusted than many humans. If there is a hereafter, and I believe there is, that old faithful dog is there; for if man has a never dying soul, then all other intelligent life must be immortal, so the grand old dog's soul must be roaming the elysian fields, happy through all eternity, possibly waiting for his earthly charges to meet him and carry on.

"WANTED, A WIFE." During a rather extensive practice of forty-two years, it has been my good fortune to run into some rather odd experiences, both amusing and pathetic. Personally, I have observed several cases where men have advertised for a wife, some of which worked out beautifully and others became wrecks on the sands of time.

As the men in the two following cases are on the other side of Jordan and the surviving ladies have left our glorious California their stories will bear telling.

Case No. 1. There was a fairly well-to-do stingy old bachelor living in Sonoma County some years ago who got tired of trying to keep a dirty house dirtier, he longed for a kindly female of the species to minister to his numerous needs, so he placed an ad in a San Francisco paper for a wife as none of the local women who knew him would have him as a gift.

He did not have long to wait, for his glowing account of himself brought a flood of replies. So, selecting the one that promised the most, he and she exchanged several letters and a date was set for the lady to arrive by rail in his home port. All "dolled up" in his very best, he was at the station when the northbound NWP train arrived to greet her in a befitting manner.

Well, she jauntily tripped off the train and looked about to see what she could see, all expectant and jittery, a very charming up-to-date lady all in fine feathers.

Bowing and scraping with hat in hand, he advanced, greeted the lady, and introduced himself. She stood for a moment as if paralyzed or something, while the good old engine at the head of the train panted in readiness to move on north; then she opened her mouth, let out a scream that seemed to be "Oh, my God," whirled about, boarded the train, and continued her journey north, leaving the intended benedict nonplussed and crestfallen alone in his misery.

Be it known to all readers that this man was very fat and no Adonis, so you could not blame the lady for her sudden attack of cold feet. This setback did not discourage him. He tried again. The next time he arranged to meet the lady in San Francisco and this time it worked, they were duly married by a justice of the peace, and the happy couple came home in a blaze of glory and happiness.

This lady was no model of beauty, but she had craft and energy and after getting her cat-like claws on what she was after, while she hornswaggled her addlepatted hubby, one fine day when he was away on business she deftly gathered her loot together and lit out for parts unknown. It was a great score: no runs, no muffs, no children.

The doting deluded husband was a bit shocked over the situation, for he had been trimmed for a couple of thousand dollars, a lot of clothes, and other gimcracks which gave him more of a pain in the neck than did the loss of the she-devil that had made a peaceful life a round of terror.

Case No. 2. In this case the man in question was a college graduate, a gentleman in every sense of the word, who had been all in, out, and down over a love affair earlier in life and who was staging a comeback.

As soon as he had things going well he pined for the love and companionship of a good woman to make life worthwhile, so he put an ad in an eastern paper for a helpmate and in due time received several letters.

Selecting the one that pleased his fancy most, they corresponded, exchanged references, which spoke well for both, and all being satisfactory, they agreed to meet and marry. The day was set for her to arrive in what was to be her new hometown. Plans for an immediate wedding were laid. Guests were invited to a reception, nothing was over-looked. The prospective groom and his friends were all agog, some a bit jittery, but all expectant.

The ecstatically happy groom-to-be with a few of his friends were at the station to greet the lady, who proved to be a lady of culture, from the deep southland (quality folks) rather tall, nearing middle age, not beautiful but possessed of charm, dignity, and grace. Everybody, including the man of the house-to-be, loved her from the very jump.

After a whirlwind reception they were that evening united in the holy bonds of matrimony by a local devine and lived deliriously happy for many years. It was "honey this," "My love that," or "sweetheart so and so" on both sides, morning, noon, and night, such superlative devotion almost made some of the neighbors have the fantods, it was all so wonderful for each thought the other the only pebble on the beach, happy as two pups in a basket.

Their unbounded happiness and prosperity continued for several years until the husband and lover was taken ill and went the way of all flesh to his eternal home on high. The lady, heart-broken, returned to the land of her birth to grieve over her lost love and the few short years of her blissful matrimonial venture.

THREE JACKS. This story goes back to those Archaic days when fine ladies did not smoke cigarettes, drink cocktails, or park themselves against a bar and whoop it up, also it was in the days of horse-drawn gooseneck drays by means of which freight was moved about town. The three men of this sketch were not named Jack but they were outstanding figures in the life of the town. They were Charles B. Proctor, Harry Truitt, and his elder brother, Roland K. Truitt.

The Truitt family first located at Pine Flat in the days of the boom of the Socrates and other quicksilver mines in that area. The family moved to town and R.K. purchased the old opera house from Ransom Powell on Center Street, revised it so it could serve as a theatre, skating rink, and assembly hall for political meetings and grand balls.

The Truitts originally came from Texas and R.K. had served two years with the Confederate Army when he either got "religion" as some say, or because he had been

The Truitts, from left to right: Sol, Harve, Roland K., John, and Harry.

severely punished for being AWOL, he did desert the Confederate cause, made his way north and joined the Union Army, serving with them until the end of the war. On account of his having been a rebel soldier he was not eligible for membership in that time-honored institution, the GAR, but always paraded with them on state occasions, dressed in civilian garb.

He was a picturesque character, a man of high ideals, and one of the leading citizens of the day. C.B. Proctor and Harry Truitt composed a draying firm who did a good business with fine teams of Clydesdale horses and old-fashioned gooseneck drays. Both could hold their quota of brandy and sugar, both could swear for minutes on end without repeating themselves. They did so much "cussing" just as a matter of habit that the air about them smelled of sulphur. Proctor could out-swear Truitt, but both were pastmasters in the art of lurid expletives, and many of the real good ladies of the town would plug their ears when they drove their ponderous drays and gigantic horses about town lest their modesty be shocked or their ears singed.

Most of the town boys looked up to them as paragons because of their ability to work hard, smoke hard, drink hard, and cuss harder than anyone else in town. To ride about town with them, to help load and unload the great drays, and be able to bask in the glory of their lurid language was supreme bliss.

C.B. Proctor was also snare drummer in the old Healdsburg Band, the Leurch Band, and for years was in the superlative Sotoyome Band. He could just make that drum sing. There was none to compare with him when it came to manipulating that percussion instrument, the snare drum. There was a daughter, May, who was almost as good as her father when it came to playing the small drum. As quite a small girl, she used to march in the band drumming along with her father, and was he proud—strutting peacocks would have hung their heads in shame, he so far outclassed them with his pride in his little girl as she rubby-dub-dubbed, ratty-tat-tatted, and rrrooollled her drum while she marched beside her noble sire.

Harry Truitt, besides being a good all-around Healdsburger, was also famous for being the progenitor of a charming daughter, Eva, a cute little girl who was very much afraid that she would be an old maid. She liked the boys and all the boys liked her. She was a honey.

In passing it might be mentioned that R.K. Truitt was a man of family having a daughter, Emma, three sons, Eugene, Ellie and another whose name has slipped into oblivion, due to the flight of time and possibly to arterio-sclerosis, which comes to us all as we travel that great highway, "The Path of Life."

JAMES WOOD. James Wood, a Healdsburg pioneer, a great-grandfather on my mother's side, was born not far from the Hudson River in New York in April 1807, and was reared in those hard-headed days before and after the War of 1812. All his life he followed the teachings and customs of his youth; honest to a fault, hard headed as a block of granite, and believing that good old Biblical doctrine of an eye for an eye and a tooth for a tooth.

In fact, he was so determined that he would pull his own teeth when they bothered him or became loose. With a pair of old-fashioned dental forceps, once to my small boy's horror and amazement, I saw him do just that to an offending molar. He was so set in his ways that when all his teeth were gone via his own extraction method, he would not have artificial teeth. The last few years of his life he subsisted on spoon victuals and buttermilk. Perhaps it was the buttermilk that kept him so active during his declining years.

The old man was an expert mechanic and millwright, and when he framed a building, putting it together with mortise and tenon and hand-made oak dowels, a cyclone could not rip it apart. In 1872, with his two sons, Calvin and Senica, and two other carpenters erected the hotel at Skaggs Springs which still stands in good condition and has been used every day of the year during the sixty-nine years of its useful existence.

He built many buildings in and about Healdsburg the same efficient way, and some are still standing monuments of the handy work of an able craftsman. When first known to me, he was in his seventies and was willing to work, pray, or fight as the occasion demanded, but he would rather cut off his right hand than cheat, wrong, or defraud anyone. Meeting Fred McConnell, attorney, on the street the other day, he told me that as a small boy he lived across the street from the Mulgrew family in Santa Rosa and remembered Grandfather Wood very distinctly and recalled many of his eccentricities—telling of the following method of keeping the birds out of a favorite cherry tree each season when its boughs were laden with ripening fruit.

Birds in the garden or fruit trees had always been an obsession with him; as a result he had become an expert with a sling shot while living in the Tucker Street home in Healdsburg. In Santa Rosa the birds would raid a large Black Tartarian cherry tree in the Mulgrew yard shortly after the break of day, too early for the old fellow to arise and initiate his anti-bird campaign, so to keep the birds scared he rigged a fairly large old hand bell in a top branch, carried a rope from his bed upstairs out through a window to the limb where the bell was hung.

The old man would wake at the first peep of day and at few minute intervals while yet in bed he would give the rope a yank, set the bell to ringing, and scare the birds. Although the noise disturbed some of the neighbors it kept the pesty birds out of his cherry tree until he could get up and at them with his trusty sling shot. For several years until he crossed the great divide he saved the cherry crop by this effective if odd method.

Another of the old boy's quirks, according to Attorney McConnell, was to wear a skull cap to which were attached several sleigh bells and as he walked about, shook his head, or swatted flies, they would magically jingle much to his own satisfaction and the mirth of the neighbors. The old man died at the age of eighty-eight, proud of his voluminous snow white beard, bald head, and combatative spirit, fighting grimly to the last. And thus endeth another lesson in ancient history and human psychology.

THE LADY GOT "SOUSED." This story goes way back to the very early history of Healdsburg, some time in the '60s, when the town was but a village, for I heard it when a very small boy and then it was almost legendary.

It seems that in one of the rural districts, not far from town, on a ranch lived a couple who loved their toddies. The man of the house operated a small still for pleasure and profit, making his own hootch, yet he did not think it right and proper that his good wife should get swacked every time he went to town, as he could do all the drinking for the family. He tried out every known scheme to hide from his partner in life his potent home-grown nose paint, before he went to town every Saturday to market his products and buy supplies.

His efforts were all in vain for she would ferret out the hiding place no matter where it might be, and when he came home after a hard day's work at the bars and stores in town he would find his energetic helpmate in a blissful state of intoxication. There was a great live oak tree in their back yard, and a brilliant idea penetrated his dome of thought. He would swing his keg of liquor out of her reach high in the branches of the great tree. Then it would be beyond her reach, for she could not climb the tree.

The next time, before making his regular trip into town, he put into effect his wonderful plan and with the aid of a ladder and a set of blocks and tackle he swung the ten-gallon keg some thirty feet off the ground to a limb of a tree. "Now," he reasoned, "she can't get that and when I come home tonight Honey will be sober as a judge and

I will be happy." Chuckling with glee he went to town and told some of his old cronies about his brilliant plan to insure his wife's sobriety.

Being convinced of the success of his plan he stayed in town rather late, getting home about sundown. To his chagrin he found his good spouse flat on the ground under the tree, pickled to the gills. He looked up into the tree, there was the keg high and dry, but on glancing at the ground under the keg he saw the washtub with all his stock of good corn liquor in it.

And this is how it all happened. When Honey spied the keg out of her reach and no way to get it down or at it, she placed the old wooden wash tub on the ground directly under it. She was not to be fooled by her foxy husband. She was not going to be cheated out of her Saturday jag. She went into the house and brought forth his good old eight-square rifle he called "meat in the pot," which had come with them across the plains from Missouri and, taking careful aim—for she was a center shot with rifle or six-gun—she shot a hole in the lowest portion of the keg and the firewater slowly dripped into the tub. She proceeded in spite of her husband's precaution to indulge in her Saturday spree. Determination and perseverance will always overcome insurmountable obstacles.

A JOKE ON F. MULGREW.

Frank Mulgrew, son of Mr. and Mrs. J.F. Mulgrew, was born in the old Tucker Street home of James Wood, along about Christmas of 1874. He was two and a half years younger than your narrator and a second cousin on my mother's side, his mother being Molly Wood.

After selling their interest in the *Healdsburg Enterprise*, John Mulgrew got into politics and moved to Santa Rosa, so Frank attended schools in the Rose City. After completing his education at the University of California, he got a position as a feature writer on one of the big San Francisco dailies. His employer sent him to several parts of the world because he was slow and efficient in his work, always getting what he went after, no matter how long it might take. When in school he would sometimes stumble and fall due to a slight impediment in his gait, which in later years he overcame. The following story was told to me by Frank himself, so it must be true.

It happened during his last year in high school. It seems that the senior class was giving a dinner and members of the class were waiting on their distinguished guests. The youth and beauty, the elite, the great and the near great, parents, teachers, trustees, and other distinguished guests of honor attended.

When the soup was being passed, Frank was about to place a cup of bouillon in front of a lady, gorgeously gowned in evening dress, when he either tripped or otherwise lost control of the cup, for with great dexterity he proceeded to pour the whole business down her v-shaped back, much to her horror and Frank's chagrin. He blunderingly offered a few million apologies and with his waiter's towel helped mop up the seeping soup. When calm was restored and the lady's clothing felt like a wet sponge next to her skin, to do himself proud, Frank reached out and took a cup of bouillon from one of his classmates passing by. Somehow in the struggle to properly balance the cup, Frank again lost his equilibrium and proceeded to dump the second cup after the first!

This was more than human patience could endure. The lady rose, her face red as a beet with anger, wheeled on Frank while he was endeavoring to offer a few million apologies in the greatest humility—for he was truly deeply grieved over the misadventure—she gave him a resounding slap with the flat of her hand, stormed out of the room followed by her escort, and went home to undress, wash off the bouillon, change to new clothing, and return to the party.

Sad mistakes do happen, and through no fault of the individual concerned. Frank told me this story about forty years ago when we were both in college. He has gone to the bourn whence no traveler returns, and is resting peacefully with his father, mother, and two brothers in Oak Mound Cemetery, and has left no heirs, so far as I know, so there is no harm telling the story.

A NEAR ACCIDENT. It was in the days when Ben Leard was city marshal, Dick Kinslow was night watchman, and each evening at 8 p.m. in winter and 9 p.m. in summer the old bell in the ancient tower in the center of the plaza would toll out the hour of curfew and all the small boys would scamper for home unless it was a special occasion or an adult was with him.

In those days there were fewer trees in the square and they were much smaller for they have grown a lot in half a century; also there was no green lawn to add to its beauty, so in the spring the wild grass grew high and in the summer it turned yellow in the sun.

It was also in the days of torch light processions, the firing of anvils, and the burning of great piles of cordwood and boxes in the middle of the streets at the four corners of the plaza together with such pyrotechnic display as the times afforded, when something was needed to rouse the enthusiasm of the benighted populace, or when some great political victory was to be ratified.

Of course the band played for pay, someone would orate, the people would shout and cheer and altogether they would have a grand and glorious time. It also happened that the local Republican party and the GAR (not an alphabetic relief bureau) were the proud possessors of an old brass smooth bore cannon with a four- or five-inch bore. This old gun was mounted on wooden wheels and must have been with Andy Jackson at the battle of New Orleans for it looked just like the guns behind the breastworks as pictured in the history books of our school days.

On the evening in question, perhaps they were celebrating the election of Benjamin Harrison as President of the United States; in addition to all the other features as previously mentioned, the old gun was being fired at regular intervals from the intersection of Powell and Center Streets. The gun would be sponged with water, dried with a swab, the powder charge inserted, some paper or rags used for wadding, the hold would be rammed home with a rammer, the touch hole filled with powder, and with a long iron rod, one end heated red hot the gun would fire and my, what a roar, it would rattle windows, shiver your timbers, and make your ears buzz.

All was going smooth as horse feathers, the noise, the fireworks, the enthusiasm of the crowd were at fever heat, the climax of the celebration was about to be reached when some smart boy, when no one was looking, chucked a rock about as big as a man's fist into the mouth of the loaded gun just to see what would happen.

The gun was fired and with the explosion there was a scream as the rock hurtled through the air just missing the bell tower, the tree tops, and the heads of the people on the sidewalk across the plaza and crashed with a sickening thud and a shower of glass through the front window and into the brick wall of the Ruffner Store, which was on the ground floor of the Odd Fellows Building. No one was hurt but a lot of folks had the scare of their lives, the old brass gun was fired no more that night and perhaps never since.

What has become of the old relic is a puzzler, for it should be among the prized exhibits of the old hometown. (Could this be the one owned by the Healdsburg City Archives at city hall as of 1965?)

A LOCAL HERMIT. In a letter from Guy H. Jackson, an old-time Healdsburger now living in North Bend, Oregon, he mentioned a unique character, an old gentleman known as André, who lived down the lane from the depot leading to the Passalacqua garden and the ten-acre ranch my father owned back in the '80s.

Shortly after Frank Passalacqua received title to his fine garden property he sold about a half-acre to Mr. André, a newcomer, and the old gentleman erected a snug little cottage and planted a flower garden which was the pride of his heart and the community; he kept it in perfect condition, raising many kinds of precious flowers.

He spoke both French and German, had a military bearing, was dapper, very polite and dignified, and perchance came from Alsace-Lorraine. Some thought he was a political exile for he never told of his past or why he came to Healdsburg, although he did have a miniature replica of his home and gardens in the old country, of which he was very proud.

Each day he would dress up in his very best. With a small market basket on his left arm and a dainty cane in his right hand he pranced up town for the mail and necessary shopping. His greatest delight was to have the ladies of the town call on him, which they did in large numbers, for he was a gracious host and would serve cakes and tea, or wine, or beer, as seemed meet and proper depending whether his guests were WCTU or otherwise. The ladies always departed with large bouquets of beautiful flowers which he generously bestowed.

Occasionally he would pick a fine bouquet and present it to some lady he liked or admired. His manners were Chesterfieldian and he was always welcome wherever he went. But he seldom entered other people's houses, just calling, leaving his gift after passing the time of day and then was on his way.

As a small boy I passed his home two to four times a day in driving cows to and from our pasture at the end of the lane, so in this way became quite friendly with the old gentleman. It gave me quite a thrill to pause and chat with him or enter his domain; have him show me his beautiful garden or partake of a cookie and a small glass of very light wine. It was exciting to be on friendly terms with so strange and mysterious a human being. What became of the old fellow no one seems to know, for such is life;

The Frank Passalacqua home on Fitch Street in 1905.

the hero of yesterday is replaced by the hero of today, only to be supplanted on the morrow by another.

A STAGE ROBBERY. Back yonder in the early '80s, when the stage line ran from Lakeport to Kelseyville and on through Tyler Valley across the headwaters of Tyler Creek, a tributary of Pieta, over the divide and by every torturous but good stage road, across Kicking Horse Creek, Hummingbird Creek, down Squaw Creek where the road at times rounded the precipitous bluffs, to the confluence of that famous trout stream with Big Sulphur Creek near the Kissack ranch, then on down past Red Hill, the old toll house, Carpenter Creek, Blue Slide, and out into the valley to the head of rail at Cloverdale. This stage line made one round trip each day, carrying passengers, mail express, baggage, sometimes fast freight.

On the date in question, the stage had reached a bend in the road where a bridge crosses Carpenter Creek, this bend hid from view the approaches from both sides of the road. The driver wasn't thinking of holdup men, when out from the brush stepped two masked men with leveled revolvers, and ordered, "Hands up." All they wanted was the Wells Fargo treasure box, which, according to a tip they had received, should contain a few thousand dollars in gold and silver. All they got for their trouble was eleven watches on their way to San Francisco to be repaired. The whole haul wouldn't be worth $200 as they were mostly silver watches without their chains.

The stage was ordered on and came into Cloverdale to report the holdup. Ab Crigler was deputy sheriff in Cloverdale at the time. He reported to the sheriff's office by telegram, was ordered to swear in a deputy and round up the robbers. He selected Sam Allen, who was a known crack shot with an old .44 Winchester. Crigler was armed with only a Colt's .45 six-gun. Allen took his Winchester with him, which showed his wisdom. They drove out in a buckboard to the spot where the holduptook place, tied their team to a tree, found the empty express box, and began looking for signs that might have been left by the robbers in their flight. Indications were that they had gone down the bank to Sulphur Creek and crossed to the opposite side and had scaled the high bluff which at that point was some 300 to 400 feet above the bed of the stream.

These road agents figured on laying low on top of this cliff until nightfall, when in the darkness they could make their getaway with their puny loot. They didn't figure on swift pursuit or the keen eyes of Sam Allen, who spotted them lurking among the rocks on top of the cliff. Crigler, from the opposite side of the canyon, in the name of the law, called on them to throw down their arms, raise their hands above their heads, and surrender, enforcing his command with his aimed Colt's .45. At this, one robber rose from behind the rock and shot Crigler dead. As he fired, Sam Allen, with lightning rapidity, raised his rifle, pulled the trigger, and sent a heavy slug from the old Winchester into the robber's right eye, the bullet going clean through his head. Truly his light was blown out. He pitched forward over the cliff and lodged on a rock behind a poison oak bush about halfway down the cliff, too dead to skin.

The other robber, seeing what happened to his pal, rose from his position and tried to even the score by taking a shot at Sam Allen, but he never got a chance to pull the trigger for again Sam, with rapid and accurate aim, shot the pistol out of the robber's hand. The heavy bullet plowed along his forearm, shattering both bones, emerging near the elbow and plowing a furrow along his right side along a rib, lodging near his spine. This highwayman, though desperately wounded and now unarmed, for his pistol fell into the creek, fled along the ridge back of the ranches on the east side of the river road, gaining the railroad after dark, near Asti. This he followed at night, laying up under culverts during daylight.

Four days later he was captured in an exhausted condition from loss of blood, hunger, and exposure, between Litton Springs and Healdsburg. He was taken into custody and while awaiting trial died as a result of infection, which set into the untreated wounds. Had he lived, he would have surely been hanged, for back in those days the hard-headed citizenry had little sympathy for criminals, stage robbers, and others of that ilk.

The old-timers were practical men. Few were mollycoddle(rs), of the belly-aching, sob-sister variety, who today feel sorry for the poor unfortunate law breakers who commit wanton crimes of violence. Some are even such sapheads they will send flowers to evil-doers.

Wells Fargo and Company presented Sam Allen with a beautiful .45 Winchester, suitably engraved, for his expert marksmanship. Ab Crigler was given honorable burial in token of his bravery. He was a good man and paid with his life the mistake of not first shooting the culprit through the head with a Winchester and arresting him afterward, which was safe, sane, and logical. This method in vogue in the wild west of our childhood often saved the taxpayers long and expensive trials. In the early days a good honest-to-God vigilance committee would have sat in solemn judgment, heard the evidence, and unanimously condemned the criminal and without further ceremony would have taken him out and hung him to the first tree they could find. Sam Allen lived in Cloverdale for many years, was a fine and respected citizen who passed to his eternal rest only a few years ago. This is another true story of events in Sonoma County.

A DOG POWER PUMP. When John Grater (a short, fat, jolly, glad-handed German) and his wife (a rather forceful Irish lassie with a foghorn voice) built the Union Hotel, now known as the Plaza Hotel, they installed some very old-country ideas, such as using a Chinese gong to call the guests to meals. Three times a day Grater would get out this ancient oriental tocsin, beating it in the lobby, the bar, and out in front of the building on the sidewalk. The sound of this gong would reverberate and echo through the old hotel, up and down the street, and across the plaza. In fact, on clear days it could be heard for blocks. How its music made people's mouths water, for the Graters were famous for the tempting viands they spread upon their table, and the price was 25¢ for a big husky meal. Being thrifty and not wanting to depend on outside sources for a water supply, Herr Grater had a deep well behind the hotel and installed a good-sized pump to lift the water into a large tank atop a tankhouse.

For the motive power he had a large cage or wheel-like contraption, treadmill fashion, connected to the pump and two very large dogs which, when water was needed, were placed in this exaggerated squirrel cage. Round and round it would go as the dogs walked within the wheel. This gave them exercise and helped them earn their daily bread, for each dog could consume enough food for four men. The dog food cost nothing, for there were plenty of scraps from each meal served, to more than feed the dogs, cats, and pigs which were kept in a pen behind the hotel.

The Graters were great hosts, set a bountiful table, ran a well patronized bar, made every nickel count, were honorable citizens, and waxed fat and rich. Thus another lesson in ancient history, with a bit of comparison as to the cost of grub today and what was sixty or seventy years ago.

A VANISHING RACE. When I was a small boy, my mother and father both told me stories of their childhood days which are as vivid today as when related over sixty years ago. The first ten years of my mother's life was spent on a large farm near Cornellville, Green County, New York. Her family name was Schermerhorn, being Holland Dutch. In those days several generations, including in-laws, uncles, aunts, and cousins, all lived together in a great house with many bedrooms, with a large kitchen, and dining room to accommodate a large family of many relatives or, sometimes, in several small houses on the same estate.

Each and every one from grandmother on down to youngsters had their work or chores to do, so none was idle, for they raised their own cattle, sheep, hogs, and poultry; grew flax and all other farm products; carded, spun, wove, and made all their own cloth, sheets, blankets, comforters, and bedspreads from wool and flax; also their clothing was hand-sewed. They plucked their geese to make feather beds and pillows, tanned leather, and made their own harness and shoes.

Every farm had its own smithy and shop, spinning-wheels, and looms; in fact, each estate was a self-containing, self-supporting, and self-sufficient unit. The cooking was done before great open fireplaces, on spits or in large iron kettles, and the baking was accomplished in a dutch oven by the fire or in a large brick oven.

Every fall the whole family would go into the woods and gather bushels of wild nuts and store them for the coming season. They had great cellars, some above, some underground, in which to store fruit, vegetables, and cured meats to last through to the next spring when nature again began to produce an abundance for another year. They made their own maple syrup and sugar, ground their own meal and flour from home-grown grains—wheat, corn, rye, buckwheat, and oats. In addition to cured meats in the late fall they would kill beef, sheep, and hogs which were allowed to freeze solid before being stored in a cold cellar which was packed with snow or cakes of ice from the millpond, and when meat was needed it was cut off with a saw, then thawed and cooked.

Bread, cakes, cookies, doughnuts, and pies would be baked or fried once a week to supply the family needs. Around the holiday season, at least fifty pies would be baked in one day. Some of these would be frozen for future use. At the proper season, wild berries would be gathered, gallons at a time, and either dried or preserved for winter use. They had their own orchards and made good hard cider and apple butter.

Great separate barns for horses, cattle, sheep, and hogs would be filled with hay, fodder, pumpkins, beets, and grain for the feeding of all the stock which was always housed during cold or stormy weather.

They had no labor-saving gadgets, all work was done by hand from seed time to harvest and back to seed time again. They made all their own farm machinery and worked from before daylight until bedtime, holding family prayers each evening; attended church every Sunday; observed all holidays in a manner befitting the occasion. Had parties of all kinds, including husking bees, quilting parties, and log raisings, sleigh rides, summer and winter sports, for they were monarchs of all they surveyed, they had no labor problems or strikes to deal with.

When members of the family became too old or otherwise incapacitated to do their share, they were not kicked out or placed on public charity, but were given every consideration as honored members of the family unit.

This was all in the good old days before old age pensions, social security, and other modern forms of so-called cockeyed social reforms. Then here's to the memory, fortitude, and patience of our hardworking forbears whose example and precept are well worthy of our imitation. And thus endeth another lesson in ancient history.

ADAM AND EVE. In the first chapter and 17th verse of Genesis we read "So God created man in his own image, in the image of God created he them: male and female created he them," and a little further on in the same book we find they were named Adam and Eve, a beautiful story in a few words.

Atop the crest of the range of hills southeast from town stand two giant fir trees. In my boyhood days these two living monuments to the handiwork of the Almighty were known as Adam and Eve, and just between them stood two lesser trees of the same specie named Cain and Abel. It has been more than fifty years since having the pleasure of standing under these beautiful old trees and intimately viewing their sublimity, yet I never pass up or down the Redwood highway without taking a glance at them as they stand sentinels of the ages against the sky line. Sad to say they appear to be dying for their upper branches are falling away leaving the stark poles pointing to the eternal blue, like milestones along the pathway of life.

All things in nature must reach maturity and crumble into dust, so it will be with these two grand old trees for no doubt they have seen a thousand years of sunshine and storms pass over them. There is quite a grove of smaller trees about their bases and under their spreading branches was a beautiful cool glade where fifty years ago and more the young folks used to hold picnics, and what fun we did have. It is safe to say that there has not been a picnic there in over twenty or thirty years for the art of walking is becoming lost and the simple pleasures of these past days have lost their appeal.

Who first named these old trees Adam and Eve and their offspring Cain and Abel is shrouded in the haze of the past for my mother told me they were known by those names when she first came to Healdsburg in the spring of 1870, so some old-timer must have been a bible student with a poetic imagination to have so endowed them.

Trees like all things in nature declare the Glory of God and attest to His wisdom, majesty, and power. To stand under some of the great trees and look up through the foliage is as inspiring as to stand in some sacred temple, for the trees in ancient times were our first temples, fills one's being with a feeling of reverence for the mightiness, grandeur, and sublimity of nature.

We who inhabit this section of this grand old world should occasionally turn our eyes to the east and view these stately old trees and as the morning sun lights up the hill crest we might do well to bow our heads as did the Indians and offer up our thanks to the Great Spirit, the giver of all good, who holds the universe in the hollow of His hand and express appreciation for the manifold blessings and comforts we enjoy, including life, liberty, and the pursuit of happiness.

Dr. Shipley's Clover Leaf Catarrh Remedy

William C. Shipley was a man who liked to combine professional training with commercial endeavor. Shortly after making the decision to settle in Cloverdale and open a medical practice, he formed a partnership with fellow physician Harry C. Trask, in the drug store business. The two men called their establishment Clover Leaf Pharmacy, probably in deference to their host town, but at the same time hopefully endowing the enterprise with good luck.

It was especially convenient that Dr. Trask, in addition to being a medical doctor, was also a graduate in pharmacy and thus experienced in the mystery and art of the apothecary. Large block letters reading "DRUGS" were attached to the wall above the awning of their false-front building, and a pole sign at curbside announced the store's name to passing pedestrians and vehicles. The Clover Leaf Pharmacy was located on the west side of the town's main thoroughfare, West Street (now Cloverdale Boulevard), a few doors south of Second Street. It opened for business in early 1909.

In addition to prescription service and nationally advertised nostrums, most druggists of the day offered some useful medicines packaged under their own "private label." And so it was that Dr. Shipley, in the spring of 1911, first promoted his own brand of toothache drops, corn eradicator, poison oak remedy, stomach and liver bitters, and what was to become his most successful product, "Clover Leaf Catarrh Remedy."

"Catarrh" (rhymes with guitar) had been a household word for at least a century, referring to those annoying conditions characterized by increased mucous flow, especially in the nose and throat. The most common forms of catarrh were conditions that are recognized today as seasonal rhinitis, hay fever, and head cold. But lumped into the same category for merchandising purposes were influenza, mumps, croup, and the dreaded catarrh of the bladder. A modern diagnostician would identify the latter malady as an infection of the genito-urinary tract, treatable with sulfonamides and antibiotics.

Dr. Shipley wisely chose to do battle with catarrh of the head and chest. His remedy was an oily liquid laden with volatile substances that would penetrate into the nasal and bronchial passages after being smeared in the nostrils with a finger, or sprayed there

RJ Kelton afflicted w/catarrh from childhood but never did know that word for it.

152

The "Catarrh Cowboys," played by Dr. Shipley's son and friends, appeared in this ad for Shipley's Clover Leaf Toilet Cream and Clover Leaf Catarrh Remedy.

with an atomizer. The good doctor's daughter-in-law recalled in later years that the odorous ingredients also effectively penetrated into every passageway of the house whenever it was used. Reference to a druggist's formulary of the period indicates that Shipley's preparation probably contained the following: oil of eucalyptus, oil of wintergreen, menthol, and thymol, dissolved in a mineral oil base.

Clover Leaf Catarrh Remedy sold for 50¢ a bottle and was available from "leading druggists" or sent postpaid by the manufacturer. It was put up in a small (one ounce) clear glass bottle, stoppered tightly with a cork, and identified with a colorful red and green paper label. When his bottles were blown at the glassworks, Dr. Shipley ordered a custom-lettered mold that caused the product's name to be embossed on one side of the oval bottle.

Embossed bottles were popular with early druggists and medicine makers because occasional wet conditions during shipping or storage caused labels to separate from bottles; it was the embossed name that preserved identification of the product and salvaged its marketability.

A statement on the Clover Leaf Catarrh Remedy label reads, "Guaranteed by Clover Leaf Pharmacy under the Pure Food and Drugs Act, June 30, 1906 . . . Serial No. 32187." This was Dr. Shipley's federally registered guaranty that his medicine was not adulterated or misbranded. It also implied that any dealer functioning merely as a sales agent would be provided immunity from charges filed against the manufacturer for adulteration or misbranding. A guaranty statement of this style was required on labels of all proprietary medicines made in the United States from January 1909 to May 1916.

An eye-catching photo of Dr. Shipley's young son, Billy, posing in makeshift Wild West garb with two of his pals, was used on an advertising postcard about 1911. The caption suggests that the little cowboys, with Billy on the right, are asking the viewer to try Clover Leaf Catarrh Remedy and Clover Leaf Toilet Cream.

Dr. Shipley sold his retail pharmacy business in November 1911, agreeing to its merger with the Grant & Riechers Drugstore down the street next to the post office. The deal allowed, however, that he retain the name "Clover Leaf Pharmacy" for use on the line of proprietaries that continued to be manufactured in Cloverdale.

By 1913 the Clover Leaf Pharmacy was incorporated, with William C. Shipley as president, H.I. Baker as vice-president, Jotham L. Sedgley as secretary, and Charles B. Shaw as treasurer. Their product line at that time consisted of the Catarrh Remedy, Toilet Bleaching Powder, and Toilet Cream. Correspondence in the collection of the Cloverdale Historical Society reveals that Dr. Shipley was still selling his Clover Leaf Catarrh Remedy to at least one loyal customer as late as 1920.

—Frank A. Sternad, Pharm. D.

A History of The Sonoma County Historical Society

Having read the accounts written by Dr. Wm. Shipley, it is easier to understand how his interest would cause him to want to preserve the history of Sonoma County for posterity.

This interest led to the formation, in 1948, of the Sonoma County Museum and Art Gallery Association, with Dr. Shipley as president. The organization was quite active and many meetings were held, many plans were explored. Considerable enthusiasm was engendered and the organization flourished. After a half dozen years or so, when no immediate results to build or buy a museum building developed, apathy took the place of enthusiasm and the activities slowly came to a stand still. (Burton Travis, William Borba, and Edward Fratini were associated with Dr. Shipley in this organization.)

This static condition existed for some time; then in 1962 a proposal was made by Mrs. Walter Nagle to form a new organization and a meeting was held June 10, 1962, by an interested group of eight people. This resulted in the birth of a new organization called the Sonoma County Historical Society. Officers were elected and a committee appointed to set up bylaws.

The purpose of the society primarily was to have a broader basis than just a museum and art gallery. Their purpose and objects were to operate as a Sonoma County historical service, to assist in naming streets, roads, parks, and buildings with historical names, to keep the public informed of families, etc. Also, if possible, to support a historical museum where articles and documents and books of historical interest and value could be exhibited.

The first officers elected were as follows: president, Mrs. Edward H. Connor, Santa Rosa; vice-president, William S. Borba, Sebastopol; treasurer, Burton M. Travis, Forestville; secretary, Mrs. Wm. Lippincott, Santa Rosa; recording secretary, Jeanne Thurlow Miller, Santa Rosa. Trustees in addition to the officers were Edward Fratini, Petaluma; Edwin Langhart, Healdsburg (not present at first meeting); Harvey Hansen, Santa Rosa; and Mrs. Walter Nagle (as guest.)

The officers and members pledged full support of President Connor, and her enthusiasm, vigor, and vitality were an inspiration to all. An indefatigable worker recognizing no obstacle as insurmountable, she assumed the leadership with grace. With the generous help of a dear lady, Mrs. Ruby Jewell Codding Hall and her son Hugh Codding, on behalf of the Codding Foundation, an educational and cultural trust, the sharing of a building for museum purposes, at 557 Summerfield Road, Santa Rosa, was offered to the society at a rental fee of $1 a year.

Many members assisted in putting the museum in readiness (notably Mr. Travis) and it was opened publicly on January 19, 1964. Dr. and Mrs. Earle Rogers contributed generously to its success, keeping it open each Sunday from 1:30 to 4:30 p.m.

The society is incorporated and is a bona-fide concern. A journal, issued quarterly to a rising membership of around 300, is edited by Mrs. Connor. Membership is $2.50 annually, or $50 for a life membership.

At the second annual dinner meeting January 15, 1965, at the Coddingtown Saddle and Sirloin Restaurant, at the beginning of the third official year of the existence of the society, new officers elected were William S. Borba, president; Edward Fratini, vice-president; Burton M. Travis, treasurer; Mrs. Edward Connor, corres. secretary; Edwin Langhart, recording secretary. The trustees were Dr. Earle Rogers, Santa Rosa; Mrs. James Weed, Monte Rio; Mrs. Cecil Fewel, Guerneville; Everett Chaney, Sebastopol; Mrs. Robert McClelland, Cloverdale; Miss Edna Cooper, Sonoma; and Mrs. Jeanne Miller and Harvey Hansen, Santa Rosa.

On April 5, 1965, a Rural Cemetery Association (for the care of the early day pioneer cemetery on Franklin Avenue, Santa Rosa) was formed. Dues are $1 a year, and the chairman for 1965 is Mrs. Robert J. McMullen, Santa Rosa.

The Sonoma County Historical Society has enjoyed the generosity of many members, companies, and organizations, without whose help the measure of progress and success would not be possible. For this the society is most grateful. The society eagerly serves the whole county in keeping our history alive and at home where it belongs.

Our beloved Sonoma County is deserving of this consideration, and if everyone will serve in some way, we will be able to carry on.

—Burton M. Travis, Treasurer
June 1965

INDEX